UNITED STATES OF AMERICA
RIGHTS FOR ALL

Amnesty International Publications

AI Index: AMR 51/35/98
ISBN: 1-887204-15-6

First published in October 1998 by
Amnesty International Publications
1 Easton Street
London WC1X 8DJ
United Kingdom
http://www.rightsforall-usa.org

Copyright:
Amnesty International
Publications 1998

Original language: English

Printed by John D. Lucas Printing, Baltimore, MD.

Library of Congress Catalog Card Number:98-87689

UNITED STATES OF AMERICA RIGHTS FOR ALL

Amnesty International USA
322 Eighth Avenue
New York, NY 10001

CONTENTS

Glossary

ABA	American Bar Association
ACA	American Correctional Association
ACLU	American Civil Liberties Union
AI	Amnesty International
AIM	American Indian Movement
American Declaration	American Declaration of the Rights and Duties of Man
APEC	Asia-Pacific Economic Co-operation
APHA	American Public Health Association
AVP	Anti-Violence Project
Basic Principles on the Use of Force and Firearms	UN Basic Principles on the Use of Force and Firearms by Law Enforcement Officials
Body of Principles	UN Body of Principles for the Protection of All Persons under Any Form of Detention or Imprisonment
BOP	Federal Bureau of Prisons
BPP	Black Panther Party
CAP	Citizens Advisory Panel
CCA	Corrections Corporation of America
CCRB	Civilian Complaints Review Board
CIA	Central Intelligence Agency
Convention against Torture	UN Convention against Torture and Other Cruel, Inhuman or Degrading Treatment or Punishment
Crime Control Act	Violent Crime Control and Law Enforcement Act
CRIPA	Civil Rights of Institutionalized Persons Act
DC	District of Columbia
DEA	Drug Enforcement Agency
DRC	Democratic Republic of the Congo
EXCOM	Executive Committee of the United Nations High Commissioner for Refugees
FBI	Federal Bureau of Investigation
GAFE	Mexican Air Mobile Special Forces Group
GAO	General Accounting Office
IACHR	Inter-American Commission on Human Rights
ICCPR	International Covenant on Civil and Political Rights
ICJ	International Court of Justice
IIRIRA	Illegal Immigration Reform and Immigrant Responsibility Act
IMET	International Military and Education Training

INS	Immigration and Naturalization Service
LAPD	Los Angeles Police Department
LASD	Los Angeles Sheriff's Department
MCC	Maximum Control Complex
NAACP	National Association for the Advancement of Colored People
NATO	North Atlantic Treaty Organization
NCAVP	National Coalition of Anti-Violence Programs
NCCHC	National Commission on Correctional Health Care
N-COPA	National Coalition on Police Accountability
NGO	Non-governmental organization
NYPD	New York City Police Department
OAS	Organization of American States
OC spray	Oleoresin Capsicum spray
OSCE	Organization for Security and Co-operation in Europe
Ottawa Convention	Convention on the Prohibition of the Use, Stockpiling, Production and Transfer of Anti-Personnel Mines and on Their Destruction
Pcdos	Post-Conviction Defender Organizations
PERF	Police Executive Research Foundation
SHU	Security Housing Unit
SIS	Special Investigation Squad
SOA	School of the Americas
SPC	Service processing centre
Standard Minimum Rules	UN Standard Minimum Rules for the Treatment of Prisoners
The Beijing Rules	United Nations Standard Minimum Rules for the Administration of Juvenile Justice
UK	United Kingdom
UNHCR	Office of the United Nations High Commissioner for Refugees
UMOPAR	Bolivian Mobile Patrol Unit
UN	United Nations
Universal Declaration	Universal Declaration of Human Rights
USA	United States of America
1951 Refugee Convention	UN Convention relating to the Status of Refugees
1967 Protocol	UN Protocol relating to the Status of Refugees

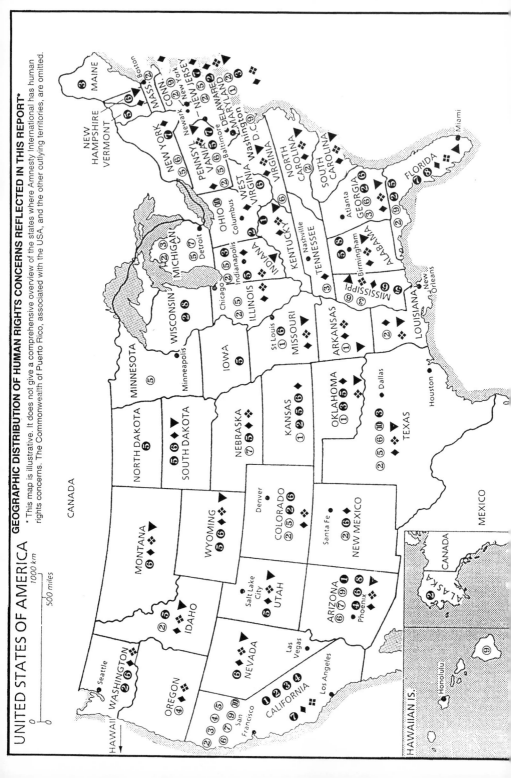

UNITED STATES OF AMERICA

GEOGRAPHIC DISTRIBUTION OF HUMAN RIGHTS CONCERNS REFLECTED IN THIS REPORT*

* This map is illustrative. It does not give a comprehensive overview of the states where Amnesty International has human rights concerns. The Commonwealth of Puerto Rico, associated with the USA, and the other outlying territories, are omitted.

KEY TO MAP

❶ Misuse of electro-shock weapons reported

❷ Use of remote-control electro-shock stun belts reported

❸ Concerns over conditions in 'supermax' prisons

❹ Concerns over health care for detainees

❺ Children may be held in adult prisons or jails

❻ No jail inspection program

❼ Concerns over conditions of detention of asylum-seekers

❽ Use of chain-gangs

① Legislation criminalizes consensual sexual acts between adults of the same sex

② Cases cited of brutality by police or federal agents

③ Death by hogtying reported

④ Ill-treatment with OC (pepper) spray reported

⑤ Cases cited of racist police practices

⑥ Ill-treatment in prisons or jails reported

⑦ Prison or jail violence reported (including rape and sexual assault)

⑨ Abuse of restraints reported (including on pregnant women)

⑩ Misuse of CS gas in prisons and jails reported

◆ Legislation provides for the death penalty

❖ Executions carried out since 1990

▼ Legislation allowing the death penalty for juvenile offenders

1

RIGHTS
FOR ALL:
Introduction

"I believe that everywhere, people aspire to be treated with dignity... to give voice to their opinions... to choose their own leaders... to associate with whom they wish... to worship how, when and where they want. These are not American rights or European rights or developed world rights. These are the birthrights of people everywhere."

US President Bill Clinton, June 1998

The USA was founded in the name of democracy, political and legal equality, and individual freedom. However, despite its claims to international leadership in the field of human rights, and its many institutions to protect individual civil liberties, the USA is failing to deliver the fundamental promise of rights for all.

Anthony Baez was playing football in the street with his brothers one December evening in New York in 1994. Their football accidentally hit a parked patrol car. An infuriated police officer grabbed Anthony and held him round the neck, then other officers knelt on his back as he lay face down on the ground. Anthony choked to death. It emerged that the officer had a long history of brutality — there were at least 14 prior complaints against him — yet he was still on duty. He was put on trial but acquitted.[1]

Tragically, the story of Anthony Baez is not an isolated incident: the US Justice Department receives thousands of complaints of police abuse each year, which many regard as but the tip of an iceberg.

There is a persistent and widespread pattern of human rights violations in the USA. This is not to say that federal, state or local authorities pursue policies deliberately designed to repress particular groups or violate human rights. Rather, it is to recognize that in the wide variety of jurisdictions across the country, practices persist which result in

---

[1] The officer was convicted on federal civil rights charges in June 1998 and had not been sentenced at the time of writing.

real and serious abuses. Some arise from individual misconduct, encouraged by an institutionalized failure to hold officials accountable. Others result from inadequate systems of control or an outright refusal to recognize or respect international standards for human rights protection. In some cases, economic policies and political trends are creating conditions in which these violations are becoming more widespread and increasingly severe.

This report focuses on several areas where the authorities have failed to prevent repeated violations of basic human rights: the right to freedom from torture and cruel, inhuman or degrading treatment, the right to life and the right to freedom from arbitrary detention. It shows that police officers, prison guards, immigration and other officials in the USA are regularly breaching their own laws and guidelines as well as international standards. It shows that the authorities have failed to take the necessary action to punish and prevent abuses, and that US government policies and practices frequently ignore or fall short of the minimum standards required by the international community.

Systematic brutality by police has been uncovered by inquiries into some of the country's largest urban police departments. In each case the authorities had ignored routine abuses. In each case police officers had covered up misconduct by fellow officers, hiding behind a "code of silence". Across the USA, people have been beaten, kicked, punched, choked and shot by police officers, even when they posed no threat. The majority of victims have been members of racial or ethnic minorities. Many people have died, many have been seriously injured, many have been deeply traumatized. Each year local authorities pay out millions of dollars in compensation to victims, yet successful prosecutions of police officers are rare.

Behind the walls of prisons and jails[2], largely hidden from outside examination, there is more violence. Prisoners are particularly vulnerable to human rights abuses, and more than 1.7 million people are incarcerated in the USA. Some prisoners are abused by other inmates, and guards fail to protect them. Others are assaulted by the guards themselves. Women and men are subjected to sexual, as well as physical, abuse. Overcrowded and underfunded prisons, many of them privatized, control inmates by isolating them for long periods and by using

---

[2] Prisons generally hold people sentenced to more than one year; jails hold people before trial, awaiting sentence, or serving a sentence of generally less than one year. Amnesty International uses the term "prisoner" to cover people held in both prisons and jails.

methods of restraint that are cruel, degrading and sometimes life-threatening. Victims include pregnant women, the mentally ill and even children. The weakness of independent scrutiny, together with a public mood demanding harsher treatment of offenders, have created a climate in which such human rights violations can occur.

The USA was built by immigrants and claims to stand against oppression and persecution. Yet the US authorities persistently violate the fundamental human rights of people who have been forced by persecution to leave their countries and seek asylum. As if they were criminals, many asylum-seekers are placed behind bars when they arrive in the country. Some are held in shackles. They are detained indefinitely in conditions that are sometimes inhuman and degrading. New legislation increases the risk that refugees may be sent back to a country where their life or liberty is in danger — a denial of a fundamental principle of international law.

In another denial of the rights to life and freedom from cruel treatment, more than 350 prisoners have been executed since 1990. A further 3,300 people await their deaths at the hands of the US authorities. Fuelled by politicians making inflammatory and false claims about the death penalty, the rate of executions and the number of crimes punishable by death has relentlessly increased. International human rights standards aim to restrict the death penalty; they forbid its use against juvenile offenders, see it as unacceptable punishment for the mentally impaired, and demand the strictest legal safeguards in capital trials. In the USA, the death penalty is applied in an arbitrary and unfair manner and is prone to bias on grounds of race or economic status.

In all these areas — the conduct of police, the treatment of prisoners and asylum-seekers, and the death penalty — Amnesty International calls on the USA to bring its laws and practices into line with international standards.

There lies the problem. International human rights standards exist for the protection of all people throughout the world, and the USA has been centrally involved in their development. Some are legally binding treaties; others represent the consensus of the international community on the minimum standards which all states should adhere to. While successive US governments have used these international human rights standards as a yardstick by which to judge other countries, they have not consistently applied those same standards at home. In some areas international standards offer greater human rights protection than US domestic law, but the US authorities have refused to recognize the primacy of international law. The USA has been slow to agree to be bound by important international and regional human rights treaties: it is one of only two countries which have failed to ratify the UN Convention on the Rights of the Child. (The other is Somalia.) Even when the USA has ratified human rights treaties it has often done so only half-heartedly, with major reservations. For example, it has reserved the right to use the death penalty against juveniles, expressly forbidden by the International Covenant on Civil and Political Rights (ICCPR).

Beyond the USA's own borders, US government policies have often led to human rights being sacrificed for political, economic and military interests. During the Cold War, countless unarmed civilians lost their lives at the hands of forces trained, equipped or directed — overtly or covertly — by the USA. The USA has continued to use international law and intergovernmental systems when they serve US foreign policy interests, but has sometimes discarded or condemned these systems when they are perceived to run counter to its interests.

The USA dominates the global market for arms and security equipment exports. It has supplied, and continues to supply, arms, security equipment and training to governments and armed groups that commit torture, political killings and other human rights abuses in countries around the world.

Within the USA, federal and state laws protect a wide range of civil rights. Legislation bars race, gender or other discrimination in areas of employment, housing and education. US law affords protection in the areas of freedom of speech, religion, association, and expression. A series of safeguards protects the right to a fair trial. Individuals have the right to sue state officials directly in state or federal courts for violations of their constitutional rights — a remedy not available in many countries. There is also a well-used right to seek legal injunctions to end abusive practices. The federal government itself can prosecute officials for civil rights violations and seek injunctions to change unconstitutional practices. Recent legislation has increased the powers of the federal government to ensure human rights protection in a number of areas.

Yet, despite these safeguards, serious human rights violations continue to occur in the USA. How and why is this, and what can be done to prevent violations in the future?

Ultimately, when a society fails to care what happens to some of its members, believes that certain human beings have forfeited their human rights because of their actions, or fails to hold officials to account for their misdeeds, then it creates the conditions in which human rights violations can thrive. Human rights are universal and indivisible; all human rights should be enjoyed by all people. But people cannot fully

The federal system

The USA is a federal republic of 50 states and the District of Columbia where the city of Washington — the seat of US government — is situated. Each of the 50 states exercises a significant measure of self-government. Each has its own constitution, elected government, laws, courts and correctional facilities.

The federal government has jurisdiction over matters of national interest, including defence, foreign affairs and internal security. The federal penal code deals with offences which come under federal jurisdiction, such as treason and other crimes against national security. Federal laws and courts apply to all US citizens.

The US Supreme Court is the highest judicial court and acts as interpreter of the US Constitution. Its nine Justices are nominated by the President, approved by the Senate and serve for life.

The founders of the USA instituted a strict separation of powers between the executive, the legislature and the judiciary. This was designed to ensure that no one individual or group became overly dominant within the government. The result is that presidential initiatives may be blocked by hostile Congressional votes, new Acts of Congress may be vetoed by the President, and the Supreme Court may hold either to be unconstitutional.

Although states have independence in framing legislation, their laws and practice must be compatible with the basic rights guaranteed by the US Constitution. Many of the most important fundamental rights and liberties are contained in the Amendments to the US Constitution, particularly the first 10 Amendments — adopted between 1789 and 1791 — known as the Bill of Rights.

exercise their political rights or safeguard their civil freedoms if they are marginalized from society by poverty or discrimination.

This report concentrates on the US authorities' actions in several specific areas, but these cannot be seen in isolation from the political, social and economic context in which they take place.

Divisions and inequalities

The USA has the most powerful economy in the world. Yet it is beset by social problems including unemployment, disease and violent crime. There are extreme disparities of wealth and power; an estimated nine per cent of the nation's children live in extreme poverty and many within US society are destitute. Millions of Americans do not have access to quality educational opportunities or comprehensive health care; some 35 million Americans lack medical insurance. Drug and alcohol addiction are rife.

© Jim Bourg/Reuters

Four-year-old Demi Gonzalez among thousands of empty shoes owned by, or representing, the victims of gun-related violence in the USA, during a protest outside a gun factory in Springfield, Massachusetts.

Homicide is the leading cause of death among young black people in the USA today.[3] One contributory factor is the prevalence of firearms: more than 200 million handguns, rifles, shotguns and high-powered weapons are currently in circulation in the USA. The USA's current response to crime centres on the imposition of harsher punishments, including mandatory minimum prison sentences, the prosecution of juveniles as adult offenders, longer prison terms and the removal of parole options for a range of crimes, especially drugs offences. As a result, the USA now puts a higher percentage of its population behind bars than almost any other country on earth.[4] The number of people in US prisons and jails tripled between 1980 and 1996 to more than 1.7 million. The number of women in prisons and jails has quadrupled over the same period. Another 3.8 million people are on probation or parole.

The poor often do not receive adequate legal counsel to preserve all their rights. Although indigent defendants have the right to a lawyer in criminal cases, they are often assigned inexperienced and inadequately funded attorneys. The problem is particularly acute in the complex area of death penalty procedural law. It is a cruel irony that those on trial for their lives sometimes receive the most deficient legal representation. Federally funded legal aid for the poor in civil cases has been drastically cut by Congress in recent years.

Despite serious attempts this century to overcome racism, the USA has not succeeded in eradicating the discriminatory treatment of blacks (African Americans), Latinos and other minority groups, including Native Americans, Asian Americans and Arab Americans. According to estimates, up to one third of all young black men are in jail or prison, or on parole or probation.[5] Black people are three times less likely to be employed than whites with similar qualifications. In practice, schools remain segregated as many blacks and, more recently, Latinos are effectively confined in inner-city ghettos where poverty, crime, overcrowding and poor housing conspire to deprive them of opportunity. In the

---

[3] Robert J. Sampson and Janet L. Lauritsen, "Racial and Ethnic Disparities in Crime and Criminal Justice in the United States," in *Ethnicity, Crime and Immigration*, Ed. Michael Tonry, University of Chicago Press, 1997.

[4] E. Currie, *Crime and Punishment in America*, Metropolitan Books, New York, 1998.

[5] A national study found that 23 per cent of black males aged 20 to 29 were in prison or jail, or on probation or parole; some state and city studies have reported far higher proportions of young black males under the control of the criminal justice system. See M. Tonry, *Malign Neglect; race, crime and punishment in America*, Oxford University Press, New York, 1995.

criminal justice system there is widespread concern that drug laws in particular, although racially neutral on the surface, are not enforced equally against black and white offenders, although the reasons for this are disputed. Whatever the reasons, the effect of the "war on drugs" has been to increase the proportion of black and Latino people in prisons and jails.

The US authorities have often responded with hostility to new immigrants. This is sometimes prompted by public opinion, inflamed by politicians' targeting of already vulnerable groups. In 1996 Congress enacted the Illegal Immigration Reform and Immigrant Responsibility Act which prevents immigrants (including asylum-seekers) from challenging abusive practices and policies of the Immigration and Naturalization Service (INS) in court.

Despite the strength and achievements of the women's movement, and the legal prohibition of gender discrimination, women in the USA continue to suffer discrimination and violence. Many are abused in custody by state officials, and many more suffer violence such as battering and rape at the hands of individual men in circumstances where local, state or federal authorities are insufficiently responsive. For women of colour, the problems of racism are compounded by gender and economic discrimination. Their opportunities to gain redress, for example, if abused by police or prison officials, are lessened by poverty and social marginalization.

In 39 states, gay men and lesbians can be legally dismissed from their jobs because of their sexual orientation. While crime rates have recently fallen across the USA, reports of violence against gay, lesbian, bisexual, transgendered and HIV-positive people have increased.[6] Twenty states have "anti-sodomy" laws which criminalize consensual sexual acts between adults in private.[7] In 1986 the US Supreme Court upheld one such law in Georgia on the grounds that negative "majority sentiments about the morality of homosexuality" justified the law's

---

[6] New York City Gay and Lesbian Anti-Violence Project, *Anti-Lesbian, Gay, Bisexual and Transgendered Violence in 1997 — a report of the National Coalition of Anti-Violence Programs*, New York, 1998.

[7] National Gay and Lesbian Task Force Institute, *Capital Gains and Losses: A State by State Review of Lesbian, Gay, Bisexual, Transgender and HIV/AIDS Related Legislation in 1997*, Washington DC, 1997. Arkansas, Kansas, Maryland, Missouri and Oklahoma prohibit sodomy only between consenting adults of the same gender; 15 other states ban some sexual acts between consenting adults, generally all sexual acts between those of the same gender and some acts between heterosexuals.

restrictions, despite the constitutional right to privacy. The law is commonly viewed as a legislative condemnation of gay people.

Although the right to freedom of thought and expression is well-established in US law, some people appear to have been targeted because of their political beliefs or activities. More than 30 military personnel were imprisoned in 1991 and 1992 for conscientious objection to the war against Iraq, and were adopted by Amnesty International as prisoners of conscience.

Geronimo ji Jaga (Pratt), former leader of the Black Panther Party (BPP) in Los Angeles who was sentenced to life imprisonment for murder in 1972, was released on bail in 1997. Amnesty International had repeatedly called for a review of his case on the grounds that he may have been denied a fair trial because of his political activities and beliefs. In the 1970s the BPP was the primary target of a Federal Bureau of Investigation (FBI) covert counter-intelligence program aimed at US political groups believed to threaten state security. Geronimo ji Jaga was finally granted a retrial in March 1997 (which had not taken place by mid-1998) when a court ruled that prosecutors had suppressed evidence that might have exonerated him. However, the Los Angeles District Attorney has appealed against the decision to overturn his original conviction.

Leonard Peltier, a member of the American Indian Movement (AIM), was given two life sentences in 1977 for the murder of two FBI agents on the Pine Ridge Reservation, South Dakota, in 1975. The killings occurred during a gun battle between Native Americans and government agents in which both sides suffered fatalities. Amnesty International believes that Leonard Peltier may have been denied a fair trial on political grounds; the trial judge refused to allow the defence to introduce evidence of serious FBI misconduct relating to the intimidation of witnesses. Leonard Peltier is still in prison and all legal appeals have been exhausted. Amnesty International has called for a special executive review of the case in view of continuing concern about the fairness of the legal process.

Amnesty International has also questioned the treatment of Puerto Rican independence supporters imprisoned in the USA. In March 1998, for example, Amnesty International wrote to the Federal Bureau of Prisons expressing concern about the conditions in which Oscar López Rivera was held in Marion Federal Prison and about claims by his attorneys that he had been singled out for punitive treatment because of his political affiliations.

Campaigning for human rights

Civil and political rights in the USA have been fought for, and won, after sometimes bitter battles. For 130 years after ratification, the Bill of Rights was an expression of aspirations which were denied to whole communities. Indigenous peoples were slaughtered, forced off their lands and had their cultural traditions destroyed. Slaves were "non-persons", who were whipped, branded, imprisoned and hanged without trial. Slavery was finally abolished in 1865, but racial segregation remained legal until the 1960s, underpinning a system in which black

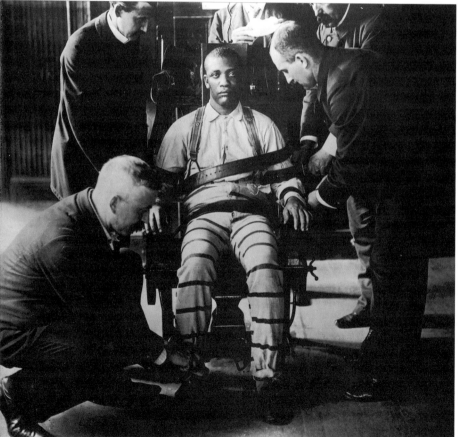

© Impact Visuals

The electric chair in use in 1900. The history of the death penalty in the USA shows how any criminal justice system can be vulnerable to personal or social prejudice.

people faced discrimination at work, at school and at the hands of the police and criminal justice system. Women were denied the right to vote until 1920, and continued to face gender discrimination.

At various points in the 20th century many groups have been denied their civil rights. Workers have been arrested and killed for labour union activities. Immigrants have been deported for their political views. Members of minority religions have been persecuted. During "Red scares" after both World Wars, the civil liberties of many were violated in the name of the very freedoms being denied them. For nearly four decades, the notorious House Un-American Activities Committee conducted an inquisition into the political beliefs of those it suspected of communist sympathies.

The middle years of this century saw concerted attempts to improve human rights within the USA. The civil rights movement of the 1950s and 1960s forced federal and state governments to remove the shackles of legal segregation and to give blacks in the southern states access to the ballot box. The Supreme Court decision in *Brown v. Board of Education* (1954) outlawed school segregation and in 1964 the Civil Rights Act banned segregation in public places such as hotels and restaurants and on transport. Black people and their allies fought tirelessly for equal treatment and rights, often at great personal cost. From the 1960s onwards, a vigorous and extensive women's movement has campaigned for women's rights at every level.

Despite this long and proud tradition, surveys suggest that today many in the USA are unfamiliar with the rights they possess, and do not appreciate that the Constitution and the Bill of Rights are there to protect everyone in the USA from abuse of power by the government. There is often popular support for restricting or ignoring certain provisions in the Bill of Rights. Recent initiatives by Congress (such as *habeas corpus* reform and the Prison Litigation Reform Act of 1996), impede the ability of federal courts to intervene when rights are violated.

There is a pressing need to safeguard the rich legacy of civil rights in the USA and to demand at least the minimum human rights protection enshrined in international human rights standards, especially on behalf of those least able to defend themselves.

A vast and diverse network of human rights activists and defenders is dedicated to that task; some are long-established, some new, amongst them religious and secular, local, state-wide and national. Many work to improve the living conditions of particular disadvantaged groups, others focus on strengthening the legal protection of those who suffer discrimination or abuse. The US human rights constituency represents and works for the rights of women, racial and ethnic minorities, religious communities, the poor, people with disabilities, gay men and lesbians, children, juvenile offenders, immigrants, refugees and others. Their role is vital both in securing rights through litigation and advocacy, and in increasing public awareness and understanding of a whole range of human rights issues.

Much of this report is based on information from such human rights groups. Amnesty International researchers have also conducted more than 18 research visits to the USA over the past three years, carrying out on-site visits and interviews. Other sources include government agencies, court documents, academics, lawyers, and victims and their relatives. We extend our thanks to all those who provided information and assistance.

This report is part of Amnesty International's contribution to the continuing efforts of the US human rights community. In the 50th

A shelter for the homeless, Memphis, Tennessee. Human rights are universal and indivisible: all human rights should be enjoyed by all people. In the USA, poverty afflicts millions.

© Lance Murphey/AP/The Commercial Appeal

anniversary year of the Universal Declaration of Human Rights, Amnesty International members around the world have been raising awareness of the rights it enshrines and mobilizing support for its values. An integral part of the continuing effort to promote human rights for all is Amnesty International's campaign against human rights violations in the USA. It is time to recognize the breadth of human rights concerns in the USA, and to make human rights protection a central issue in public policy debate. This report sets out specific recommendations to enhance respect for human rights. They include increasing the accountability of the police by setting up effective oversight and monitoring mechanisms; establishing enforceable standards for the treatment of prisoners, including steps to prevent sexual abuse of women and a ban on the use of remote controlled electro-stun belts; an end to the execution of juvenile offenders and the mentally impaired; stopping the detention of asylum-seekers in city and county jails; ratifying, in full, international human rights treaties; and adopting a code of conduct to prevent US arms and equipment being used to commit abuses elsewhere in the world.

The USA is an immensely powerful nation; it has a corresponding responsibility to take a lead by living up to its human rights promises. These promises are to be found in the USA's own laws and in international human rights standards, including the Universal Declaration of Human Rights with its vision of a world free from fear and want. However, the promise of universal human rights cannot be fulfilled if the rights of large numbers of human beings are disregarded: the rights of the poor and marginalized; the rights of minority groups; the rights of criminal offenders; the rights of asylum-seekers; the rights of those beyond US borders but affected by US policies. Human rights belong to everyone, or they are guaranteed to no one. This is why we need human rights for all.

2

UNIVERSAL HUMAN RIGHTS: International standards

The international community has adopted minimum standards to govern the conduct of states. These are based on the precept that human rights are an international responsibility, not simply internal matters. International human rights standards articulate the criteria against which the conduct of any state — including the USA — should be measured.

US treaty obligations

The USA has ratified the following international human rights treaties. It is therefore legally bound to comply with them. (There are other treaties which the USA has not yet ratified, and in some cases the USA has filed reservations asserting its intention to ignore certain provisions — see Chapter 7.)

The *International Covenant on Civil and Political Rights* (ICCPR) protects fundamental rights: the right to life; the right to freedom of expression, of conscience, and association; the right to be free from arbitrary arrest or detention; the right to freedom from torture or ill-treatment; the right to a fair trial.

The *Convention against Torture and Other Cruel, Inhuman or Degrading Treatment or Punishment* (Convention against Torture) requires the prohibition and punishment of torture in law and in practice. States must initiate investigations whenever there are reasonable grounds to believe that torture or cruel, inhuman or degrading treatment or punishment has been committed, and must bring those responsible to justice. The Convention forbids the forced return of any person to a country where they would risk being tortured.

The *International Convention on the Elimination of All Forms of Racial Discrimination* obliges states to eradicate racial discrimination, including in the judicial system.

The *Convention relating to the Status of Refugees* (1951 Refugee Convention), adopted in 1951 and the *Protocol relating to the Status of Refugees* (1967 Protocol) define who is a refugee, and therefore entitled to international protection. In 1968 the USA acceded to the 1967 Protocol, by which it undertook to apply Articles 2 to 34 of the 1951 Refugee Convention.

Other international standards

Many human rights requirements are contained in standards which have been adopted by the international community, but which are not in the form of treaties. Although these standards do not technically have the legal power of treaties, they have the moral force of having been negotiated by governments, and of having been adopted by political bodies such as the UN General Assembly, usually by consensus. The USA played a major part in drawing them up, and agreed that they should be adopted.

The *Universal Declaration of Human Rights* (Universal Declaration) is a universally recognized set of principles which identifies human rights — civil, cultural, economic, political and social — vital to everyone's well-being.

The UN *Body of Principles for the Protection of All Persons under Any Form of Detention or Imprisonment* (Body of Principles) contains an authoritative set of internationally recognized minimum standards, applicable to all states, on how detainees and prisoners should be treated.

The UN *Standard Minimum Rules for the Treatment of Prisoners* (Standard Minimum Rules), set out generally accepted good principle and practice for the treatment of prisoners. In 1971 the UN General Assembly called on all states to implement these rules and to incorporate them into national legislation.

The UN *Safeguards guaranteeing protection of the rights of those facing the death penalty* restrict the use of the death penalty in countries which have not yet abolished it. Among other protective measures, they prohibit the execution of juvenile offenders, pregnant women, new mothers or the insane. They provide that capital punishment may only be carried out after a legal process which gives all possible safeguards to ensure a fair trial, including adequate legal assistance. In 1989 the UN Economic and Social Council recommended that states eliminate the death penalty for people suffering from mental retardation or extremely limited mental competence.[1]

---

[1] Resolution 1989/64, UN Doc: E/1989/INF/7.

The *United Nations Rules for the Protection of Juveniles Deprived of their Liberty* establish minimum standards to protect young people in detention or prison, including a requirement that juveniles deprived of their liberty, as a last resort, must be segregated from adult inmates.

The UN *Code of Conduct for Law Enforcement Officials* governs the conduct of police officers, prison officials and all other people involved in law enforcement. It states that law enforcement officials must uphold the human rights of all people. They may use force only when strictly necessary and only to the extent required for the performance of their duty.

The UN *Basic Principles on the Use of Force and Firearms by Law Enforcement Officials* provide, among other things, that the use of force must be proportionate to the threat faced and that firearms may be used only in self-defence or to defend others against an imminent threat of death or serious injury. In any event, intentional lethal use of firearms is restricted to situations where it is "strictly unavoidable in order to protect life".

The UN *Principles on the Effective Prevention and Investigation of Extra-Legal, Arbitrary and Summary Executions* require that any killings that might be extrajudicial executions are promptly and impartially investigated.

The UN *Guidelines on the Role of Prosecutors* contain standards to ensure that prosecutors in criminal proceedings act in an impartial and fair manner, respecting and protecting human dignity and upholding human rights.

The UN *Basic Principles on the Role of Lawyers* provide that everyone facing criminal proceedings should have effective access to competent legal assistance, and requires governments to provide sufficient funding and other resources to provide legal counsel for the poor and other disadvantaged people.

The UN *Basic Principles on the Independence of the Judiciary* require both professional judges and lay judges to be independent from any interference, pressure or improper influence.

The *American Declaration of the Rights and Duties of Man* (American Declaration), was adopted in 1948 along with the Charter of the Organization of American States (OAS). The American Declaration is the cornerstone of the inter-American system of human rights protection, and all member states of the OAS are obliged to observe the fundamental human rights that it enshrines.

3

POLICE BRUTALITY: A pattern of abuse

Four young men in a van — three black and one Latino — were driving along the busy New Jersey Turnpike in April 1998 when they were stopped by two New Jersey state troopers. They were on their way to university basketball trials. The van accidentally rolled backwards, making an officer fall over. The police opened fire, and three of the young men sustained multiple gunshot wounds. The officers said they had stopped them for driving above the speed limit, but the men denied this and claimed they had been targeted because of their race. One of the troopers involved in the shooting had been involved in at least 19 prior incidents in which it was alleged he had stopped vehicles because of the occupants' race.

There is a widespread and persistent problem of police brutality across the USA. Thousands of individual complaints about police abuse are reported each year and local authorities pay out millions of dollars to victims in damages after lawsuits. Police officers have beaten and shot unresisting suspects; they have misused batons, chemical sprays and electro-shock weapons; they have injured or killed people by placing them in dangerous restraint holds.

The overwhelming majority of victims in many areas are members of racial or ethnic minorities, while most police departments remain predominantly white. Relations between the police and members of minority communities — especially young black and Latino males in inner city areas — are often tense, and racial bias is reported or indicated as a factor in many instances of police brutality.

Police officers are responsible for upholding the law and protecting the rights of all members of society. Their job is often difficult and sometimes dangerous. Experience from around the world shows that constant vigilance is required to ensure the highest standards of conduct — standards necessary to maintain public confidence and to meet national and international requirements.

In the USA, despite reform programs in several major police departments, the authorities still fail to deal effectively with police officers who have committed abuses. The disciplinary sanctions imposed on officers found guilty of brutality are frequently inadequate, and officers are rarely prosecuted for excessive force. The "code of silence" — in which officers fail to report brutality or cover up abuses — commands widespread loyalty, contributing to a climate of impunity. Although there has been pressure on police departments to become more publicly accountable in recent years through independent oversight mechanisms, these remain inadequate or wholly absent in many areas.

There is no reliable national data on the excessive use of force by police, and local reporting systems are patchy and often unreliable. Such data is essential to enable the authorities to take effective action. Since 1994, the federal government has been legally required to collect national data on police use of excessive force, but Congress has failed to provide the funding necessary for it to do so.

Amnesty International believes that police forces throughout the USA must be made more accountable for their actions by the establishment of effective monitoring mechanisms.[1] National, state and local police authorities should ensure that police brutality and excessive force are not tolerated: all allegations of police abuse should be promptly, fairly and independently investigated and those responsible brought to justice. Instead of simply paying compensation to victims, emphasis should be placed on stopping and preventing the abuses.

Violations of standards

Standards of conduct for police officers are set out under the UN Code of Conduct for Law Enforcement Officials and the UN Basic Principles on the Use of Force and Firearms by Law Enforcement Officials. These provide, among other things, that law enforcement officers should use force only as a last resort and that the amount of force must be proportionate to the threat encountered and designed to minimize damage and injury. Many US police departments have guidelines which broadly conform to these standards. Most large departments set out a scale of force levels, ranging from verbal persuasion and hands-on force, to the

---

[1] More than 17,000 police agencies operate in the USA, each with their own codes of practice and methods of recording and investigating abuses. These include over 12,000 municipal police departments, over 3,000 county police and sheriff departments, state and federal police agencies, and around 1,000 special police agencies (such as air and transport police).

use of non-lethal weapons, impact weapons and deadly force. However, in many instances these guidelines are disregarded and police officers have used levels of force entirely disproportionate to the threat faced.

Most complaints of police brutality involve excessive physical force by patrol officers during the course of arrests, searches, traffic stops, the issuing of warrants, or street incidents. Common forms of ill-treatment are repeated kicks, punches or blows with batons or other weapons, sometimes after a suspect has already been restrained or rendered helpless. There are also complaints involving various types of restraint hold, pepper (OC) spray, electro-shock weapons and firearms.

Police shootings

The use of deadly force by law enforcement officers is regulated by international human rights standards and by US law. Article 6 of the ICCPR states that no one shall be arbitrarily deprived of life. The UN Basic Principles on the Use of Force and Firearms provide that firearms should be used with restraint and only when absolutely necessary to prevent an imminent threat of death or serious injury. Yet Amnesty International knows of

© AI

Shu'aib Abdul Latif, a 17-year-old unarmed teenager shot dead by New York police in January 1994. According to an eye-witness, he was shot without warning during a police raid.

dozens of police shootings which appear to have violated these standards.[2]

Police shootings are reported to have declined overall since the 1970s, as agencies have moved to adopt tighter guidelines and training.[3] Many departments now have policies which broadly meet international standards.[4] Despite this, some officers still use firearms in unwarranted circumstances, and officers involved in controversial shootings are often shown to have been inadequately monitored or disciplined. Unarmed suspects have been shot while fleeing from minor crime scenes; mentally ill people have been shot when they could have been subdued by other means; victims have been shot many times, sometimes after they had already been apprehended or disabled.

Police officers are often in difficult situations where they may believe that their lives or those of others are in danger. However, controversial shootings occur with alarming regularity in certain common sets of circumstances. A leading police expert has stated that the absence of "clearly defined standards and training" means that state and local police officers "are left to improvise when motorists race away from them, when radio dispatchers tell them that robberies are in progress in local stores, when they encounter emotionally disturbed persons on down-town streets, or when distraught husbands take their wives and children hostage."[5] A lack of clear standards and training cannot excuse a lack of accountability for human rights violations committed by police officers.

---

[2] The UN Special Rapporteur on extrajudicial, summary or arbitrary executions also reported on several deaths as a result of excessive use of force by law enforcement officials, most of which were shootings. See UN Doc.: E/CN.4/1998/68/Add.3, 22 January 1998, Part IV.

[3] William A. Geller and Michael S. Scott, *Deadly Force: What We Know*, 1992, a Police Executive Research Foundation (PERF) publication, is the last major national study of police shootings. It cites research based on data from big cities showing a general decline in shootings between 1970 and the mid-to-late-1980s, linked with the introduction of stricter policies and standards.

[4] The Supreme Court set a national minimum standard in *Tennessee v. Garner* in 1985, ruling that deadly force may not be used to apprehend an unarmed, non-violent criminal suspect. This does not go as far as the strict defence of life standard under international law, but many departments have introduced stricter standards than those established in *Tennessee v. Garner.*

[5] Professor James Fyfe, Professor of Criminal Justice, Temple University, testimony to the Senate Committee on the Aftermath of Waco, October 1995, reported in *Policing By Consent.*

Disturbingly, there is no accurate, national data on the number of people fatally shot or injured by police officers — data which is essential for meaningful policy-making at both national and local levels.[6]

Systematic abuses in large cities

Most law enforcement agencies maintain that abuses, when they occur, are isolated incidents. However, in the past eight years independent inquiries have uncovered systematic abuses in some of the country's largest city police departments, revealing a serious nationwide problem. In each case the authorities had ignored long-standing and routine police brutality in high crime districts. Many of these cities have had histories of police brutality and corruption, with periodic scandals followed by reform initiatives; the emphasis on the "war on crime" in recent years has reportedly contributed to more aggressive policing in many areas.

New York: "Police brutality seemed to occur ... whenever we uncovered corruption". This was one of the findings of the Mollen Commission of Inquiry into corruption in the New York City Police Department (NYPD) in

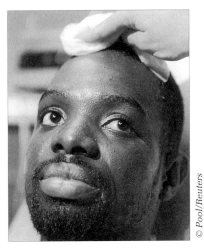

© Pool/Reuters

Abner Louima, a Haitian immigrant, suffered serious internal injuries after New York police officers allegedly beat him and one rammed the handle of a toilet plunger into his rectum at a Brooklyn police station in August 1997. Four officers were awaiting trial on federal charges of assault in mid-1998.

---

[6] The need for such data has been highlighted in *Deadly Force* (op. cit.) and later publications such as *Understanding and Controlling Police Abuse of Force*, PERF, 1995.

1994. The Commission found that the most serious abuses were concentrated in several inner-city precincts, with patrol officers protecting or assisting drug dealers, and involved in robberies, beatings, perjury and falsification of records. It also found that the NYPD had failed to monitor or discipline officers accused of brutality and that the "code of silence" had hampered internal investigations.

A 1996 Amnesty International investigation found that although steps had been taken to tackle corruption within the NYPD, police brutality remained a serious problem.[7] Local community and civil rights groups have reported that aggressive "zero tolerance" policing has been accompanied by unacceptable levels of brutality, especially toward racial minorities. The recommendations of a task force set up by the Mayor of New York to review police-community relations after the alleged torture of Haitian Abner Louima (see picture above) were largely rejected by the Mayor in March 1998.[8] Serious cases of police brutality and disputed shootings continue to be reported.

Los Angeles: Two official inquiries into policing in Los Angeles found a serious problem of excessive use of force, including beatings and unjustified shootings by patrol officers, perpetrated mainly against members of minority groups. Dozens of officers had been implicated in repeated complaints but the authorities had done nothing to investigate or stop them, suggesting a tolerance of brutality.[9] The 1991 Christopher Commission of Inquiry into the Los Angeles Police Department (LAPD) was established after the 1991 beating of Rodney King caused a national outcry, and in 1992 Judge Kolts headed an inquiry into the Los Angeles Sheriff's Department (LASD), which polices the wider area in and around Los Angeles County.

Reforms recommended by the Christopher Commission were implemented slowly, but some significant measures have been taken. In 1993 the city made the LAPD more publicly accountable by giving increased

---

[7] The report *USA: Police brutality and excessive force in the New York City Police Department* (AI Index AMR 51/36/96), based on a review of more than 100 cases since the mid-1980s, documented physical brutality, deaths in custody and unjustified shootings; most victims came from racial minorities.

[8] The recommendations included new police training programs; requiring police officers to live in the city; and abolishing the "48 hour rule" (see below).

[9] In 1992 an Amnesty International report, *USA: Torture, Ill-treatment and excessive force by police in Los Angeles, California* (AI Index AMR 51/76/92), documented abuses by LAPD and LASD officers, including beatings, shootings and the use of police dogs to inflict unwarranted injuries on suspects.

powers to the civilian Police Commission.[10] An Inspector General was appointed in 1996 to oversee the LAPD complaints and disciplinary process. The Inspector General has criticized the LAPD in a number of areas, including its continued failure to monitor adequately officers against whom complaints were lodged.

A special counsel appointed to monitor reforms in the LASD has commended the department for reducing excessive force by patrol officers through better monitoring and investigatory procedures, with a 70 per cent drop in civil lawsuits from 1992 to 1997. However, he noted a rise in brutality complaints against deputies from two inner-city police stations in 1997.[11] One of them, Century Station, is the former Lynwood area station which was the subject of a major police brutality lawsuit several years ago, involving scores of plaintiffs, some of whom were awarded substantial civil damages in 1995.

Philadelphia: In the Philadelphia Police Department in the mid-1990s, drug squad officers operating mainly in the 39th District (a poor, black neighbourhood) were accused of systematically beating and robbing suspects, planting drugs and falsifying reports. Several officers — who had operated with impunity for many years — were eventually jailed and hundreds of convictions based on the evidence of corrupt police officers were overturned.

In September 1996, the City of Philadelphia signed an agreement with three local civil rights groups[12] to implement wide-ranging reforms in the police department. This forestalled a civil lawsuit the groups were about to file. The reforms included the appointment of a task force to review recruitment, training and discipline, and improvements in reporting and monitoring police use of force, including monitoring for racial bias in discretionary police actions such as pedestrian and vehicle stops.

Pittsburgh: In February 1997, the Justice Department used new powers[13] to charge the City of Pittsburgh with tolerating a long-standing pattern of abuses by the Pittsburgh Bureau of Police, especially in black communities. The abuses included brutality, unjustified stops and searches,

---

[10] An amendment to the City Charter gave the Los Angeles Police Commission power, among other things, to appoint the Chief of Police for a (once-renewable) five-year tenure. Formerly, the Chief of Police had an unlimited term of office.

[11] 7th Semiannual Report by Special Counsel Merrick J. Bobb & Staff, April 1997.

[12] The Philadelphia chapters of the ACLU and the NAACP, and the Police-Barrio Relations Project, a community organization.

[13] Under the Crime Control Act of 1994 (see below).

and false charges against people who complained about police behaviour. Instead of going to trial, the city agreed to wide-ranging reforms through a landmark Consent Decree (court-supervised agreement), which included detailed procedures for monitoring officers' behaviour (see below).

Several other major cities have been plagued by police brutality and corruption. One of the most notorious police departments, the New Orleans PD in Louisiana, underwent a major overhaul in the mid-1990s, after more than 30 officers were arrested for crimes including extortion, murder and brutality. One officer was convicted of conspiring to murder a woman who had witnessed him beating a youth and had filed a brutality complaint against him.

There were widespread protests in Chicago in 1997 after a spate of cases involving racist ill-treatment. They included that of Jeremiah Mearday, a black teenager who suffered serious injuries after being beaten with a flashlight by two white police officers. Two officers were subsequently dismissed from the force, but complaints of brutality have continued and the internal monitoring system has been criticized as ineffectual.

As of mid-1998, federal investigations into allegations of brutality and corruption by police officers had also been conducted or were under way in Detroit, Atlanta and other areas.

Federal agents

There have been long-standing complaints of ill-treatment by Immigration and Naturalization Service (INS) Border Patrol officers in the US-Mexico border region. Serious abuses have continued since a Citizens Advisory Panel (CAP) was established in 1994.[14] They include people being kicked, punched and hit with batons, often as punishment for running away from Border Patrol officers; sexual abuse; and denial of food, water and bedding to people held in Border Patrol stations. The victims have included men, women and children. In December 1997, the INS issued an Action Plan to implement reforms recommended by the CAP in areas of complaints investigation, training and community relations.

Federal Bureau of Investigation (FBI) agents have also used unnecessary levels of force. In 1995 the government paid $3.1m in settlement

---

[14] See Amnesty International, *USA: Human Rights Concerns in the Border Region with Mexico*, AI Index: AMR 51/03/98, May 1998.

CHAPTER 3

© Jeffry Scott

A Border Patrol agent arresting a man at Nogales, Arizona

of a wrongful death claim to the family of a white separatist whose wife and son were shot dead by FBI sharpshooters during a siege in Idaho in 1992. A Justice Department inquiry found that senior officials in charge of the siege had violated federal policies on the use of deadly force. While several senior officials were demoted, no officers were prosecuted.[15] During a 51-day stand-off with members of an armed religious sect — the branch Davidians — in Waco, Texas, in 1993, federal agents pumped CS gas into a compound known to hold children as well as adults, for three and a half hours. The siege ended when fire engulfed the compound, killing over 70 men, women and children.

Patterns of brutality

"They were really beating Quentin, pushing his neck and calling him a little punk. I couldn't believe that this was happening right in front of us, and there was nothing we could do".

A witness testifying about a police assault on black high school students in
Denver, Colorado, May 1996

---

[15] A charge of involuntary manslaughter was brought under state law against one officer (after the federal authorities declined to prosecute him), but was dismissed in May 1998.

Common patterns of ill-treatment by police have been identified. Inquiries such as those cited above have consistently found a tolerance of brutality among patrol officers and supervisors in certain high crime areas. They have also found that victims include not only criminal suspects but also bystanders and people who questioned police actions or were involved in minor disputes or confrontations. For example, in Pittsburgh people were beaten for asking for an officer's number; complaining about officers' use of racist or profane language; or failing to respond quickly enough to police commands. Brutality following challenges to police authority (widely known as "contempt of cop") has been widely documented. The special counsel hired to assess reforms introduced by the LASD noted in 1997 that despite improvements there were still "too many cases of physical force in response to verbal taunts and challenges".[16]

In its 1996 report on the NYPD, Amnesty International detailed many similar cases where police officers had used excessive force in response to minor incidents, including assaulting bystanders for taking photographs or criticizing police treatment of others.

Reports of discriminatory treatment by police toward racial and ethnic minorities are common. One of the most persistent claims is that African Americans and other minorities are far more likely than whites to be stopped and searched without cause. Black people who are arrested for minor offences appear particularly liable to suffer police brutality. Johnny Gammage, a black businessman, died of suffocation while being subdued by police officers who had stopped him for a traffic violation in 1995. All the officers involved (from two suburban police departments near Pittsburgh) were white. One was acquitted of manslaughter by an all-white jury and was later promoted. Prosecution of two other officers resulted in a mistrial; an appeal by the officers against a retrial was pending at the time of writing.

Another persistent claim is that black drivers are targeted as suspected drugs offenders on the basis of so-called "race-based police profiles"— a practice so common that it is widely known as "driving while black". Court cases on the issue were being pursued in at least eight states in mid-1998.

The April 1998 shooting of three young men (see above) reinforced accusations that troopers along the New Jersey Turnpike stopped blacks or Latinos solely on the basis of race in the hope of making arrests. Claims of unjustified traffic stops along major inter-state highways have

---

[16] 7th Semiannual Report by Special Counsel Merrick J. Bobb & Staff, April 1997.

been made in other states. In Maryland in 1997 a federal court found preliminary evidence of a "pattern and practice of discrimination" in police stops of black drivers along Interstate-95. A class-action lawsuit filed in June 1998 by the Maryland branch of the American Civil Liberties Union (ACLU) was pending at the time of writing. Similar claims of racial bias in traffic stops have been made in other areas, including Philadelphia, Volusia County, Florida, and parts of Colorado, Illinois, Indiana and Texas.

In January 1997 Congressman John Conyers introduced the Traffic Stops Statistics Act into Congress, requiring the Attorney General to acquire national data about traffic stops by law enforcement officers and to publish an annual summary. The Act had been passed by the House of Representatives but was pending before the Senate at the time of writing. At least one state, Rhode Island, has passed similar legislation.

In a number of cases, young black men have been shot by police who believed them to be armed, revealing an apparent readiness to stereotype black people as potential criminals and to disregard their right to life. In November 1997 a deputy US Marshal (a federal agent) shot and wounded 17-year-old high school student Andre Burgess when he walked past an unmarked police car. The agent said he mistook Burgess' candy bar for a gun, and a grand jury acquitted him of criminal wrongdoing.

An unarmed African American man, William J. Whitfield 3rd, was shot dead in a New York supermarket on 25 December 1997 by police who said they mistook the keys he was carrying for a gun. Although the officer who shot him was cleared, it was revealed that he had been involved in eight prior shootings but had not been placed on any monitoring program. The NYPD Police Commissioner subsequently set up a monitoring system for officers involved in three or more shootings.

Black police officers themselves have long complained of the apparent stereotyping of black males as criminal suspects. In New York City alone, 23 black undercover police officers have reportedly been shot by fellow officers since 1941 after being mistaken for suspects, and others have been assaulted. Ron Hampton, a retired police officer and executive director of the National Black Police Association, confirming these concerns, told Amnesty International in 1998 that "In a training video, every criminal portrayed is black."

Car chases

Violence by police after car chases is frequently reported. A report by the ACLU of Southern California found a "troubling tendency of officers to mete out street justice by the roadside after the conclusion of a pursuit".[17] It revealed that more than 40 per cent of injuries and deaths of suspects occurred after the chase was over.

James Wilson, a white man, was hospitalized with head and facial injuries in February 1997 after being beaten by three officers in Hartford, Connecticut. The beating was captured on a police video inside a police cruiser and two officers were subsequently charged. Gil F. Webb, a 17-year-old African American, had his neck broken and suffered other injuries in March 1997, after being involved in a car crash in Denver, Colorado, in which an officer was killed. A videotape showed him being kicked by a police officer, grabbed by the arms, legs and hair and slammed twice onto a wooden board after he had been removed, injured, from his car. The officer was disciplined by losing five days' holiday.[18]

Police have shot at vehicles during and after pursuits when there was little reason to suspect that the occupants were armed or that deadly force was necessary.[19] In February 1996 an unarmed Korean man, Hong Il Kim, died after a chase that started over a minor traffic violation. Two police officers fired 20 shots into his car after it had been cornered and forced into a parking space. Five national experts in police use of deadly force who reviewed the videotape all stated that it was avoidable and that the officers had committed a series of tactical errors that cost Kim his life. However, an internal investigation by the City of Orange Police Department, California, cleared the two officers of wrongdoing or violating departmental policy.

In April 1997 Caroline Sue Botticher, an unarmed African American woman, died after police from West Charlotte, North Carolina, fired at the car in which she was a passenger when it failed to stop at a checkpoint.

Fourteen-year-old Jenni Hightower was killed in March 1998 in Trenton, New Jersey, after police fired 20 shots into the stolen car in which she was a passenger. The driver, 16-year-old Hubert Moore, was critically injured. A state grand jury declined to file criminal charges

---

[17] ACLU Foundation of Southern California, *Not Just Isolated Incidents: The epidemic of police pursuits in Southern California*, June 1996. The study looked at 12 agencies in California and found 5,766 pursuits between 1993 and 1995, with 47 fatalities and 1,240 injuries to suspects.

[18] Information from Mark Silverstein, ACLU, Colorado.

[19] According to the ACLU report cited above, despite the high rate of fatalities police vehicle pursuits were most often initiated for vehicle code violations that would not themselves justify the use of deadly force.

© Kim Kulish/Reuters

Two Riverside County sheriff's deputies were videotaped beating and club-bing two Mexican immigrants after a car chase in April 1996. The two vic-tims, Leticia González and Enrique Funes Flores, later received substantial civil damages. A protester holds a sign saying "We are human, we demand respect."

against the officers when they argued that the teenagers had tried to run them down. (One officer was reportedly hit by the car when it swerved into him after the police had fired into the vehicle.) The case is one of more than 12 New Jersey police shootings of unarmed teenagers (most of them black) in disputed circumstances since 1990.

Some police departments have introduced guidelines designed to avoid unnecessary deaths or injuries during vehicle pursuits. Many, such as the LASD, now bar police from firing at moving vehicles unless they are directly threatened with deadly force. Although police shoot-ings have often been justified on the grounds that the vehicle itself was used as a deadly weapon, some guidelines (such as those for the LASD) stipulate that officers should not remain in the path of a moving vehicle.

Civil rights lawyers have expressed concern that moves to control police conduct during vehicle chases may be undermined by a May 1998 US Supreme Court ruling. The Court ruled that police officers cannot be held constitutionally liable for deaths during pursuits unless the officer acted with intent to cause harm. This overturned a lower court's ruling that an officer was liable for depriving a teenager of his right to life by displaying "deliberate indifference" to his safety during a chase.[20]

Excessive force against the mentally disturbed

According to reports received by Amnesty International from many areas, mentally ill or disturbed people have been subjected to excessive force by police. While some disturbed individuals pose a danger, extreme levels of force have been used against people engaged in bizarre but non-threatening behaviour. For example, James Parkinson, an unarmed mentally ill man seen running naked around a swimming pool in June 1996 in Fairfield, California, died after police sprayed him repeatedly with OC (pepper) spray, hit him several times with an electric taser gun and shackled him face-down.

Police officers have shot distraught people armed with weapons such as knives or sticks, in circumstances suggesting that they could have been subdued without lethal force. Kuan Chung Kao, a Taiwanese man who was drunk and wielding a pole in Sonoma County, California, was shot dead less than a minute after police arrived at the scene in April 1997. A Massachusetts man in a wheelchair who was trying to stab himself in the stomach was shot dead by police in November 1997 when he refused to put down the knives.

In August 1997 the City of Los Angeles agreed to pay $200,000 to the family of 18-year-old Efrain Lopez, who was shot nine times by an LAPD officer during a family disturbance. City lawyers reportedly advised settling out of court because a jury might have found that "alternative but less deadly measures should have been taken".[21] No officers were prosecuted or disciplined.

Independent police experts believe that the adoption of special procedures for dealing with emotionally disturbed individuals would prevent many unnecessary shootings. Professor James Fyfe has told Amnesty International that he has provided expert advice in at least 40 cases nationwide where the police had unnecessarily shot mentally disturbed individuals. An independent study of the Albuquerque Police

---

[20] *County of Sacramento v. Lewis.*

[21] *Los Angeles Times*, 21 August 1997.

Department (New Mexico) reported numerous shootings of the mentally disturbed and recommended that the city develop a mental health response team, which has now been introduced.[22] Some departments have adopted special procedures for dealing with the disturbed[23], others have not.

Stakeouts

There have been allegations of unwarranted shootings during police stakeouts. Particular concern has been raised about the activities of the LAPD's Special Investigation Squad (SIS), an elite surveillance squad. According to media reports, the City of Los Angeles has paid $1.9m in damages arising from SIS actions since the squad was formed in 1965. At the time of writing there were at least three civil cases pending before federal courts involving SIS officers. They included a 1995 incident in which 13 plainclothes SIS officers reportedly followed two suspected robbers, waited while they carried out a robbery, then shot one dead and seriously wounded the other. In February 1997, SIS officers shot dead three suspected robbers and a bystander: the shooting took place just after the suspects, whom the SIS had reportedly had under surveillance for a month, had robbed a bar. All the officers involved had been cleared of wrongdoing by LAPD internal inquiries.

Police stations

Suspects have been tortured or ill-treated inside police stations. In September 1997, two former officers from the Adelanto Police Department, San Bernardino County, California, were jailed for two years on federal charges, after pleading guilty to beating a suspect during questioning and forcing another man to lick blood off the floor in 1994. At the time of writing, four NYPD officers were awaiting trial, charged with the torture of Abner Louima in August 1997.

Ten men who were allegedly tortured and signed confessions in a Chicago police station remain on death row.[24] Allegations of systematic torture in one police station over a 20-year period came to light in 1989, involving at least 65 suspects who reported torture including electric shocks and having plastic bags placed over their heads. The cases were

---

[22] Eileen Luna and Samuel Walker, *A Report on the Oversight Mechanisms of the Albuquerque Police Department*, 1997.

[23] Departments which have set up Crisis Intervention Teams, trained by mental health specialists, include Memphis (Tennessee), Portland (Oregon) and Seattle (Washington).

[24] Information from G. Flint Taylor, an attorney with the People's Law Office in Chicago.

reopened by Chicago's Office of Special Investigations in the 1990s and the area's commander was dismissed. Other officers, however, were allowed to retire with full benefits.

Dangerous restraint holds

There have been numerous deaths in police custody following restraint procedures known to be dangerous. Suspects have died after being placed face-down in restraints, usually while "hogtied" (where a suspect's ankles are bound from behind to the wrists), or after pressure has been applied to the neck or chest. Such practices can severely restrict breathing and can lead to death from "positional asphyxia", especially when the subject is agitated or under the influence of drugs.

A San Diego Police Department task force identified 94 cases of "restraint-related in-custody deaths" involving hogtying or neck holds across the country in the 10 years to 1992, and concluded that the true number was likely to be significantly greater.[25]

Hogtying has been recognized as a highly dangerous procedure for at least the past decade. The New York Commission of Correction's Medical Review Board issued a report in October 1995 in which it confirmed the dangers of hogtying, and the increased risk of asphyxia in the cases of people who struggle or have taken drugs.[26] The National Institute of Justice also issued guidelines in October 1995 urging police departments to avoid hogtying.[27] However, while many departments, including the NYPD, have now banned the procedure, others continue to use it.

Hogtying was banned within the LAPD only in August 1997, despite dozens of deaths in LAPD custody since the mid-1980s of suspects who were hogtied.[28] The eventual ban was achieved only as part of the settlement of a civil lawsuit in which the city paid $750,000 to the family of a man who had died from a hogtie restraint. The

---

[25] San Diego Police Department, *Final Report of the Custody Death Task Force*, June 1992.

[26] Chairman's Memorandum No. 14-95, October 20, 1995, New York State Commission of Correction. The Review Board noted that the majority of restraint-related deaths occurred in healthy young adults, with no pre-existing heart conditions, or who had not taken fatal drugs doses.

[27] National Institute of Justice, *Bulletin on Positional Restraint*, October 1995.

[28] A list of deaths in LAPD custody between February 1985 and August 1995 issued to Carol Watson, a civil rights lawyer, by the Police Commission showed that 62 people died in police custody, of whom 48 were hogtied.

© Judi Parks

Police arresting demonstrators at a non-violent rally for "Food not Bombs"
in San Francisco, 1994.

authorities had reportedly paid out more than $2 million to settle similar cases in the previous five years.

Other police agencies in Los Angeles County continue to use the technique. In January 1997 Kenneth Callis, a black man arrested by Culver City police officers for being in possession of "cocaine parapher-nalia", died after being placed hogtied in the back of a police car. The coroner found that "positional asphyxia" was the primary cause of death.

In April 1998 a court awarded $12.9m to the family of a man who died after being hogtied by police in Lansing, Michigan. Other deaths have been reported in various parts of the country, including Athens (Georgia), Jackson (Mississippi) and Memphis (Tennessee).

During a June 1997 visit to Maricopa County, Arizona, jail officials told Amnesty International that police from the Mesa and Phoenix police departments frequently delivered suspects to the county jail "suitcased" (i.e. hogtied).

Suspects have also died from police choke holds, where pressure is applied to the neck. Many large police departments, including the NYPD and San Diego PD, now ban the use of choke holds, but there has been at least one death in New York as a result of a banned police choke hold. Other police departments still allow the use of choke holds. For example, it was reported after the death of Eli Montesinos, a Mexican visitor placed in a choke hold by an off-duty police officer in San Antonio, Texas, in 1997, that several Texas police departments had not banned choke holds.[29]

Less-than-lethal weapons

The police have a variety of so-called "less-than-lethal" weapons at their disposal, including chemical sprays, electro-shock weapons and batons. These devices are designed to stun or temporarily disable, although the risk of death is not totally eliminated.

International standards encourage the development of non-lethal incapacitating weapons, in order to decrease the risk of death or injury. However, the standards also state that these should be "carefully evalu-ated" and that "the use of such weapons should be carefully con-trolled".[30]

---

[29] *San Antonio Express News*, 13 January 1997

[30] Principles 2 and 3 of the Basic Principles on the Use of Force and Firearms by Law Enforcement Officials.

OC (pepper) spray

At least 3,000 US police departments authorize the use of Oleoresin Capsicum (OC) spray — an inflammatory agent derived from cayenne peppers. OC spray inflames the mucous membranes, causing closing of the eyes, coughing, gagging, shortness of breath and an acute burning sensation on the skin and inside the nose and mouth.

Although the spray has been promoted as a safer and more effective alternative to chemical mace or impact weapons, there is mounting concern about its health risks. Since the early 1990s, more than 60 people in the USA are reported to have died in police custody after being exposed to OC spray. While most of the deaths have been attributed to other causes, such as drug intoxication or positional asphyxia, OC spray may have been a contributing factor in some cases.

The US manufacturers of OC spray and various law enforcement surveys have pronounced it to have no verified long-term health risks. However, there have been no definitive independent studies on the safety of OC spray.[31] Some research studies have found that OC spray can be harmful to people with respiratory problems such as asthma and heart disease — conditions that may not be apparent at the time of use.[32] An internal memorandum by the largest supplier of OC spray in California concluded that serious health risks may ensue if someone is sprayed with more than a single one-second burst.[33] Many police agency guidelines allow more than this, and many police officers have breached even the more permissive guidelines.

OC spray has sometimes been applied in a deliberately cruel manner to suspects who are already restrained. In October 1997, Sheriff's deputies in Humbolt County, California, swabbed liquid OC spray directly into the eyes of non-violent anti-logging demonstrators, action Amnesty International condemned as tantamount to torture.

In Eugene, Oregon, police used OC spray against peaceful environmental protesters in June 1997. One man in a tree was videotaped being hit repeatedly by police officers and sprayed on his legs and genitals

[31] The credibility of some of the most influential reports recommending OC spray was undermined in 1996, when the author (an FBI Special Agent) was sent to prison for taking bribes from one of the country's largest OC spray manufacturers.

[32] These studies include: ACLU of Southern California, *Pepper Spray Update: More Fatalities, More Questions*, June 1995, which investigated 26 deaths from OC spray in California; research by Dr Woodhall Stopford of Duke University Medical Center, North Carolina; and research by Drs Hazel and John Colderidge published in November 1997.

[33] Cited in ACLU, ibid.

UNITED STATES OF AMERICA

© Jim West/Impact Visuals

Police using OC (pepper) spray on union members during a non-violent protest in Decatur, Illinois, in June 1994. Workers were demonstrating against a year-long lock-out of members of the United Paperworkers' Union.

after police cut open his trousers; he reportedly required hospital treatment for burns.

Monitoring of the use of OC spray by police is inconsistent, and there are no national standards. The National Institute of Justice recommended in 1994 that police departments should issue clear guidelines for the use of OC spray, including reporting and decontamination procedures. While most large police departments have guidelines and reporting procedures, many smaller departments do not. The California Department of Justice told Amnesty International in February 1998 that in the past it had recorded the number of OC spray-related deaths and injuries, but that, as of June 1996, the department "no longer requires or maintains this information".[34]

---

[34] Letter from Earma Johnson, Analyst, California Department of Justice Firearms Program, dated 26 February 1998. Following concern about the Humbolt County cases in November 1997, the Attorney General said he would review the use of OC spray in the state.

Where police departments do have guidelines on the use of OC spray, they vary widely. Many authorize the spray only if officers face a serious physical threat, but others allow it to be used more widely. The Philadelphia Police Department has introduced some of the most stringent guidelines, stipulating that the target should be at least six feet away and allowing a normal application of a half-second burst to the suspect's face, with a maximum of two half-second bursts.[35]

Electro-shock weapons

Patrol officers in some police departments are authorized to use stun guns or tasers. The stun gun is a hand-held device with two metal prongs that emit an electric shock. The taser is a hand-held device which shoots two barbed hooks into the subject's clothing from a distance; the current is transmitted through wires. In both cases a high voltage "jolt", typically 50,000 volts, incapacitates the suspect.

There have been several reported deaths following the use of such weapons. In July 1996, a 29-year-old woman, Kimberly Lashon Watkins, died after being shot by police with a taser in Pomona, California. Just five months later, Andrew Hunt Jr died when Pomona police reportedly shot him several times with a taser after he had been handcuffed.

Electro-shock weapons of the type used in the USA have been used to torture victims in countries around the world.[36] Medical research studies have shown that they can be dangerous.[37] Stun weapons have been banned for law enforcement in countries including Canada and most West European countries. As of 1995, stun guns were reportedly illegal in Illinois, Hawaii, Michigan, Massachusetts, New Jersey, New York, Rhode Island and Washington DC, as well as in some cities.

Prejudiced policing

Racism

"Police officers have increasingly come to rely on race as the primary indicator of both suspicious conduct and dangerousness. There can be no other explanation for why a police officer would consider shooting a

---

[35] Philadelphia Police Department, Directive 43.

[36] See Amnesty International, *Arming the Torturers: Electro-shock Torture and the Spread of Stun Technology*, March 1997 (AI Index: ACT 40/10/97).

[37] For example, Robinson, Brooks and Renshaw, "Electro Shock Devices and their Effects on the Human Body", Medical Science and the Law (1990), Vol. 30, No. 4, cited in Amnesty International, *USA: Use of electro-shock stun belts*, 1996 (AI Index: AMR 51/45/96).

sixteen-year-old on a bicycle. One cannot even fathom the same thing happening to a white youth. A black teenager pedalling rapidly is fleeing crime. A white teenager pedalling at the same speed is feeling the freedom of youth".

NAACP Report on Police Conduct and Community Relations,
March 1993, commenting on the case of a black teenager
shot by police after falling off his bicycle in Indianapolis, Indiana

Members of racial minorities bear the brunt of police brutality and excessive force in many parts of the USA. The over-representation of people from minority groups in complaints against the police is undoubtedly due in part to underlying social and economic inequalities: a disproportionate number of people from minorities live in low-income neighbourhoods where police activities are often concentrated in response to higher levels of reported street crime. Opinion polls have also consistently found that African Americans and other minorities in the USA have far less confidence in the police than whites and that a significant proportion believe they are treated unfairly.[38] The extent to which race is a factor in police use of improper force in the USA is hotly disputed. However, evidence of racially discriminatory treatment and bias by police has been widely documented by commissions of inquiry, in court cases, citizen complaint files and countless individual testimonies. Reported abuses include racist language, harassment, ill-treatment, unjustified stops and searches, unjustified shootings and false arrests.

The problems are not confined to inner cities. Human rights groups have documented long-standing brutality by law enforcement agents towards people of Latin American origin along the US-Mexican border and in states with large immigrant populations such as California and Texas. There have been complaints of brutality and discriminatory treatment of Native Americans both in urban areas and on reservations. Complaints include indiscriminate brutal treatment of native people, including elders and children, during mass police sweeps of tribal areas following specific incidents, as well as failure to respond to crimes committed against Native Americans on reservations.

In Riverdale, a suburb of Chicago where the proportion of black residents has risen sharply, a number of African American women were

---

[38] Recent national surveys were cited in the *National Institute of Justice Journal* in September 1997 (article by Jean Johnson). A *New York Times* poll in October 1997 found that 82 per cent of blacks and 71 per cent of Hispanics felt the police did not treat whites and blacks in New York City with equal fairness.

assaulted by white male police officers in the mid-1990s. For example, Linda Billups was stopped by police while driving home from church with her four young children in September 1993; she was allegedly manhandled, arrested and charged with several offences including assaulting an officer. All charges were later dropped, except for driving without child restraints. Dianne Overstreet was reportedly kicked, thrown to the ground and subjected to racial slurs after an officer stopped her for allegedly going through a red light in February 1994. At least eight black women were assaulted in separate incidents in two years: the officers involved represented one-third of the all-male, all-white 30 full-time officers on the force in 1993-4.[39]

Many large police departments have recruited more officers from minority groups in recent years and have introduced cultural diversity and racial sensitivity training programs. However, in many areas there remains a wide gulf between the racial composition of the police force and the local community. There is also troubling evidence of discrimination toward black or Latino officers within some law enforcement agencies. Numerous civil lawsuits have been filed by officers from minority groups alleging discrimination, including being subjected to racist slurs or passed over for promotion. Recently reported cases include a jury award of $4m in May 1998 to a former deputy marshal who claimed he had been passed over for promotion because he was black. In March 1998, a federal district court ruled that a New Jersey state trooper of Filipino origin had suffered from racial discrimination and a hostile work environment.

Young people of colour

Many communities report that the police unjustly target young black, Latino or Asian males, especially in inner cities, and automatically see them as potential criminal suspects. In Chicago and other cities, youths in particular areas, wearing certain clothes or simply out on the street, are viewed as gang members, regularly stopped by police and often ill-treated.[40] Other reports of unfair treatment include police

[39] Information provided by Standish Willis, a Chicago attorney.

[40] Amnesty International has received reports of similar "gang profiling" leading to harassment of minority youths in San Antonio (Texas), Philadelphia and Los Angeles. Delegates to a conference organized in August 1997 by the National Coalition on Police Accountability (N-COPA), an organization of religious, community and legal groups monitoring and lobbying on police issues, cited similar examples from other areas. The definition of gang membership was so broad in some areas that it also encompassed white youths, although the overwhelming majority of those targeted were people of colour.

indiscriminately taking photographs of young Asians or other minorities and placing them in "mug shot" books to be shown to victims.[41]

In Chicago, an anti-loitering law introduced in 1992 allowed police to disperse any group of two or more people loitering "with no apparent purpose" if any of them were suspected of being a gang member. According to the Illinois ACLU, some 41,000 young people, mostly African Americans and Latinos, were arrested under its provisions.[42] The law was struck down by the Illinois Supreme Court in October 1997, which ruled that it violated constitutional guarantees, including the right to freedom of movement and association. The court stated: "Such laws, arbitrarily aimed at persons based merely on the suspicion that they may commit some future crime, are arbitrary and likely to be enforced in a discriminatory manner".[43] However, an appeal by the City of Chicago against the ruling was pending before the US Supreme Court at the time of writing.

In Michigan a study found that white youths were more likely than black youths to be released at the scene of a crime if stopped or arrested, and black youths more likely to be referred to the courts. When asked why they initiated contact with a juvenile, patrol officers frequently replied that they investigated youths who looked "suspicious"; one officer defined suspicious as a "black kid in a white neighbourhood".[44]

Gay men and lesbians

Ill-treatment and harassment of gay men and lesbians by police officers is reported in many areas. Gay and lesbian victims of crime (including victims of homophobic attacks) also allege that their complaints to the police are often not treated seriously and, in some instances, are met

---

[41] According to an Asian American community organization in Philadelphia testifying at the N-COPA Conference, Philadelphia police indiscriminately photographed Asian teenagers in the early 1990s and retained some 400 photos to be shown to victims — an illegal practice unless the subjects were directly suspected of a crime. Similar practices have been alleged in other areas, including New York, Minneapolis, Denver, Los Angeles and San José.

[42] Statement issued by ACLU, 17 October 1997.

[43] *Chicago v. Jesús Morales*. The Court acknowledged that criminal street gangs posed a serious problem but noted that there were already laws adequate to deal with criminal gang behaviour.

[44] M. Wordes and T. Bynum, "Policing Juveniles — Is there bias against youths of color?", in K. Leonard, C. Pope and W. Feyerherm, *Minorities in Juvenile Justice*, Sage, 1995.

© Maurice Rivenbark/AP/St Petersburg Times

Black teenager Tyrone Lewis was shot dead by two white police officers in St Petersburg, Florida, in October 1996 after he had been stopped for speeding and allegedly refused to roll down his window. His death caused two days' rioting among the town's black community, who accused the police of racism. Tyrone Lewis was the sixth person in the town to be fatally shot by police that year.

with verbal or physical abuse.[45] Although some police agencies have tried to tackle the problem of homophobia in police ranks, the National Coalition of Anti-Violence Programs (NCAVP) documented a disturbing increase in reported incidents of homophobic violence by law enforcement officers in 1997.[46]

[45] New York City Gay and Lesbian Anti-Violence Project, *Anti-Lesbian, Gay, Bisexual and Transgendered Violence in 1996*, March 1997. "Just over half the victims who sought police assistance found the response courteous", up from the previous year, but "37% said the police were 'indifferent', and 12% said that police response was verbally or physically abusive — up from 10% in 1995".

[46] The New York City Gay and Lesbian Anti-Violence Project for the NCAVP, *Anti-Lesbian, Gay, Bisexual and Transgendered Violence in 1997*, March 1998. The report cites NCAVP statistics showing that "the number of reported offenders who were law enforcement officers increased by 76% nationally, from 266 in 1996 to 468 in 1997". The NCAVP (a coalition of victim assistance, advocacy and reporting programs for gays, lesbians, bisexual, transgendered and HIV-positive people) notes that its statistics do not purport to document the actual number of hate crimes against such people, which are vastly underreported.

Some police departments have tried to recruit more gay and lesbian police officers and to introduce training to improve relations with the gay and lesbian community. The New York City Gay and Lesbian Anti-Violence Project (AVP) reported some improvement in NYPD officers' responses to victims in 1996, due in part to the AVP's efforts in accompanying victims to report crimes, and to regular police training and lesbian/gay sensitivity programs.

The LAPD was commended in a report to the Police Commission in 1996 for having recruited officers from the gay and lesbian community and adopting other measures to combat discrimination, following settlement of a lawsuit brought by a gay former LAPD officer in 1993.[47] This was in contrast to the situation reported by the Christopher Commission in 1991, which noted widespread discrimination within the department toward gay and lesbian officers. However, the NCAVP continued to report a generally poor response from LAPD officers to victims reporting homophobic hate crimes.

There are reports in some areas of selective enforcement of laws to target members of the gay community. For example, in May 1998 civil rights advocates claimed that LAPD officers were selectively enforcing laws to harass gay men and women, including entrapping gay men into committing illegal sexual acts. In 1997 there were complaints that police in Maryland were inciting gay men to breach the state's discriminatory anti-sodomy law (which prohibits homosexuals but not heterosexuals from having oral sex and "other unnatural... practices" in private).

Sex workers

Discriminatory treatment and physical abuse by police of sex workers have been reported, although the extent of the problem is difficult to gauge as such abuses are greatly underreported.

A recent report cites a sample survey of 32 street-based prostitutes in New York City, 10 of whom said they had been sexually or physically assaulted by police officers during arrest.[48] Other complaints have included failure by officers to take reported crimes against sex workers seriously.

---

[47] Merrick J. Bobb, Report to the Los Angeles Police Commission, May 1996.

[48] Frederique Delacoste and Priscilla Alexander, eds, *Sex Work: Writings by Women in the Sex Industry*, Revised edition in press, Cleis Press, San Francisco, USA.

Investigations and remedies

Prosecutions and discipline

Successful prosecutions of US police officers for excessive force are rare, despite a range of state and federal laws punishing offences from assault to murder.[49] The standard of proof in a criminal case is high and often rests on the word of the victim (who may also be charged with an offence) against that of the accused officer. It can therefore be difficult to obtain sufficient evidence to convict unless police witnesses themselves come forward. However, civil rights and community groups have often questioned the impartiality of criminal investigations, claiming that local prosecutors are too dependent upon police cooperation in other cases to pursue cases against them vigorously.

Police internal investigations into alleged abuses have also been widely criticized as inadequate. Independent inquiries into several large police departments have found that investigations lacked thoroughness and that officers were given the benefit of the doubt even if there was corroborative evidence of misconduct.[50] Other criticisms include delays and secrecy in investigations; failure to inform victims of the outcome of police internal inquiries; and, in some areas, obstruction of the process for receiving citizens' complaints. Several inquiries, including the Christopher Commission, and surveys by organizations such as the ACLU, have found that officers frequently discourage citizens from filing complaints through intimidation, fail to inform them of available procedures and fail to provide the necessary forms.[51]

One of the main barriers to both disciplinary and criminal action is the "code of silence". There are often no independent witnesses, and officers frequently fail to report misconduct, or file false or incomplete reports to cover up abuses. It has also been reported that police officers cover up brutality by charging the victim, or even potential witnesses,

---

[49] Although there are no comprehensive national statistics on the number of criminal prosecutions against police officers, the scarcity of police prosecutions has been amply documented in research studies, media reports and civil lawsuits. In most cases reviewed by Amnesty International in which substantial damage awards were made for police misconduct, the officers had been absolved from any criminal liability.

[50] Serious failings in internal complaints systems were found by all the inquiries into major police departments mentioned above.

[51] A 1996 test by the ACLU of the complaints process in the Oakland Police Department (California), for example, found only 36.8 per cent of officers approached with a citizen complaint correctly answered questions about the complaints process.

with offences such as resisting arrest, interfering with an arrest, or assault. In some cases people are told that the charge will be dropped if they withdraw their complaints against the police.[52]

Although most police codes provide disciplinary sanctions for officers who fail to report misconduct, the procedures have not always been adequately enforced. Failure by officers to report misconduct was highlighted by the Christopher Commission in 1991 and the Inspector General for the LAPD reported in 1997 that this was still a problem.[53]

The Mollen Commission of Inquiry in 1994 found that officers who had tried to report or investigate misconduct suffered from hostility, ostracism or reprisals from colleagues and were not protected by supervisors. The code of silence continues to be a problem in the NYPD: out of nearly 100 officers interviewed during a federal investigation into the torture of Abner Louima (most of whom had been granted immunity from prosecution in return for giving evidence), only two reportedly provided investigators with information.[54]

Other barriers to successful disciplinary or criminal action include special procedural protection afforded to police officers in some departments, often won through pressure by police unions. In New York City, for example, this includes the "48 hour rule", in which officers accused of misconduct (or involved in shootings) are not required to give statements for two full working days. In addition, the statute of limitations on police disciplinary action — the time that can elapse between an incident and the start of disciplinary proceedings — was reduced in 1983 from three years to 18 months. A backlog of cases and delays in investigations by the Civilian Complaint Review Board (CCRB) has led to cases reaching this limit before officers have been subject to disciplinary action, and the cases therefore being dropped. A one-year statute of limitations applying to LAPD disciplinary action has reportedly caused similar problems.

The obstacles to establishing police misconduct mean that the majority of complaints are found to be "unsustained" or "unsubstantiated". However, even when cases are sustained, disciplinary action

---

[52] See *Understanding Police Abuse of Force*, PERF, 1995, page 77. This was also noted in investigations into the Pittsburgh, New York and Philadelphia police departments; lawyers representing complainants in civil actions have told Amnesty International that the practice is widespread.

[53] Six-month Report of Inspector General to the Los Angeles Police Commission, January 1997.

[54] *New York Times*, 5 September 1997.

against officers for brutality is frequently inadequate. The special counsel monitoring the LASD found that, while the LASD had improved its investigatory procedures, "discipline continued to be too lax for founded instances of excessive force".[55] The New York task force on police-community relations reported in March 1998 that the NYPD had taken either no action, or imposed minimal discipline, in a large proportion of complaints found to be substantiated by the independent civilian complaint review board.[56] A poor record of disciplinary action has been found in numerous police departments around the country.

Secrecy

Public confidence in the complaints and disciplinary process is further undermined by the secrecy of police internal investigations. Police departments have frequently refused to provide information to victims, their families and attorneys. They have also denied Amnesty International's requests for information on individual cases on the grounds that these concern "personnel matters" not subject to disclosure under state confidentiality laws. Attorneys representing plaintiffs in civil actions for police misconduct have also reported difficulty in obtaining information on internal police investigations. The lack of transparency in police investigations has been criticized by independent inquiries.[57]

Criminal investigations are also often shrouded in secrecy. Grand jury proceedings are not subject to disclosure in most jurisdictions. Sometimes prosecutors issue reports or statements in especially controversial cases, but this is rare, and such reports do not carry the force of an independent inquiry. In general, information becomes public only in the rare instances when there is a trial. Civilian complaint review boards (see below) are also usually restricted from giving out detailed information on specific cases.

Civil rights groups and others have also frequently reported difficulty in obtaining data that should be available under public records acts, such as information on shootings, compensation payments and

---

[55] 7th Semiannual Report by Special Counsel Merrick J. Bobb & Staff, April 1997.

[56] The task force found that 57.1 per cent of substantiated cases resulted in no disciplinary action at all; in other cases disciplinary measures were "slight" (Report to the Mayor, April 1998). The CCRB report for 1997 revealed that action was taken in only 89 cases of 276 cases referred to the police department for disciplinary action (Semiannual Status Report of the CCRB, January - December 1997, April 1998).

[57] For example, the Curran Commission into the use of force by police in New York state in 1987.

lawsuits. Some police departments now provide statistical data on the number of complaints investigated and the number of officers disciplined each year. However, the information provided varies. Many departments do not routinely issue data on the number of police shootings or deaths in custody, for example.

Identifying problems

Many police departments have failed to take action against the generally small percentage of officers who are responsible for a disproportionate number of complaints.[58] Better systems for dealing with problem, or "violence prone", officers could help prevent abuses. A growing number of departments have developed "early warning systems" for identifying and monitoring such officers. It is equally important for police departments to be able to identify patterns of concern, such as racial bias.

A Consent Decree (agreement) reached with the Justice Department in April 1997 to improve procedures in the Pittsburgh Police Department is considered to be a model program. The agreement included proposals for a computerized record of each officer's disciplinary, training and complaints history (including unsustained complaints and data on civil lawsuits), as well as data on all arrests, traffic stops, use of force incidents, and race, including alleged use of racial epithets. The agreement provides for regular independent audits and reviews of the data for potential racial bias or other patterns of concern. Some other departments have also set up early warning systems but most do not yet go as far as the Pittsburgh model.[59]

Many cities pay out huge sums of money in damages to victims of police brutality in settlements or judgments in civil lawsuits. Although civil lawsuits provide financial compensation to individual victims, they rarely serve to hold either police departments or individual officers accountable. In nearly all cases, the money is paid out of a general city or county fund.[60] Furthermore, many cities do not systematically inform

---

[58] This was found in all the major inquiries mentioned above and in other areas. In Chicago, 200 to 300 officers out of a department of more than 13,000 reportedly accumulated as much as 25 per cent of all brutality complaints (statement by G. Flint Taylor, on behalf of the National Lawyers Guild, 18 November 1997).

[59] A sophisticated monitoring system acquired by the Chicago Police Department in 1994 was reportedly shelved after opposition from the police union and was still not in use by late 1997.

[60] Amnesty International was told in May 1997 by the city attorney in Chicago that the city did not keep a record of police misconduct lawsuits separate from other claims.

police departments about civil lawsuits, or even if they do, the departments themselves fail to keep track of such cases or to record them in officers' files. Such information is vital to enable departments to monitor officers named in repeated lawsuits or accused of serious abuses.[61]

A few cities, including San Francisco, have tried to make the police more accountable by allocating a specific sum in the police budget for payouts in police misconduct cases, with any excess to come directly from the following year's police budget.

Independent oversight

There have been growing moves in recent years to introduce independent oversight of the complaints process in US police departments.

As of June 1998, there were 94 independent oversight bodies in the USA with authority to review complaints against the police, compared to just 13 in 1980.[62] The review bodies (commonly referred to as "citizen" or "civilian" review) include civilian complaints review boards; municipal offices; and individual counsel appointed to audit the internal complaints process. Three quarters of the police departments in the 50 largest cities, as well as many smaller agencies, are now subject to some form of civilian review. However, at the time of writing, the police in 12 major cities were not subject to any functioning oversight system.[63] There is also no independent civilian review of most federal law enforcement agencies, including the FBI.

There are many different models in place, which vary in effectiveness. They include systems where civilian review boards, with civilian investigators, investigate complaints and issue recommendations, and those in which the police investigate complaints, which are then reviewed by an outside civilian body. In nearly all cases, the external review systems have an advisory function, and the police chief executive remains responsible for deciding on discipline.

A major problem for many external review bodies is lack of funds and staff, sometimes reflecting a lack of commitment on the part of politicians. For example, the all-civilian CCRB, set up in New York in 1993, was allocated a smaller budget and staff than the former police-

---

[61] Although most cases are settled out of court without an admission of liability by the authorities, civil actions can be important indicators of abuse.

[62] Information provided by Samuel Walker, Professor of Criminal Justice, University of Nebraska.

[63] They include Columbus, Ohio; Sacramento, California; Fresno, California; Boston, Massachusetts (a civilian board exists on paper but is reportedly "defunct"); and Washington DC (bill to reinstate board pending at the time of writing).

dominated board. This contributed to a backlog of cases and a reduction in complaints fully investigated and sustained.[64] The complaints review board in Washington DC was allowed to lapse in 1995 due to lack of funding and an unmanageable backlog of cases.

Many external investigatory bodies have no power to order witnesses to appear, and their investigations are thwarted if the police or others refuse to cooperate.[65] For example, the Berkeley Police Review Commission had no powers to require statements from accused officers, until it was found that it could not investigate cases adequately without them. The New York Civil Liberties Union and others successfully lobbied for the CCRB to be given subpoena powers when it was established in 1993. This is particularly important as some external complaint systems have been set up in the face of strong opposition from the police or police unions, who have not always cooperated with investigations.

Some police departments have not provided adequate feedback on the final disposition of complaints. The task force on the NYPD was critical of the police department's failure to explain the reasons for its decisions not to impose discipline in cases sustained by the CCRB as "detrimental to the work of the CCRB and harmful to police community relations".[66]

Another weakness of many civilian oversight systems is that they do not have the authority to make recommendations on policy. About a third of oversight bodies are limited to investigating individual complaints. Some bodies which have such authority have reportedly failed to utilize it effectively; however, others have made regular, constructive policy recommendations.[67]

Public reporting is a vital function of independent review and accountability. However, the reports published by external review bodies vary considerably in scope and quality. The San Francisco Office of Citizen Complaints issues an annual report which includes recommendations on policy and training and a statistical breakdown of complaints

---

[64] The present Mayor of New York had opposed the creation of an independent CCRB before he took office and has been widely accused of depriving it of funds. However, in September 1997 he substantially increased the CCRB's budget and staffing following public concern about some highly publicized police brutality cases. In its March 1998 report the CCRB reported an improvement in the number of cases investigated and sustained.

[65] Only about 38 per cent of external review bodies reportedly had subpoena power in 1997.

[66] Task force report, op.cit.

[67] Examples of bodies which have made constructive policy recommendations include the San Diego County citizens review board; the San Francisco Office of Citizen Complaints; and the Denver Public Safety Review Commission.

by type, area and ethnicity of complainant, with an additional tally of the police discipline imposed against each sustained complaint. The New York CCRB reports include statistical data on the numbers of complaints by type and precinct, and the disposition of complaints. They also provide data on the race and gender of both complainants and police officers. However, some other bodies issue minimal reports or exclude important data.[68] The Ombudsman for the LASD reportedly issues no public reports.

Some citizen complaints bodies do little to publicize their operations and little is known about them. Low visibility and lack of community outreach can render the process ineffective.[69]

Most civilian review bodies only look at complaints brought to their attention, usually by members of the public. Their review generally excludes internally generated complaints. Some authorities have appointed independent auditors (such as the Inspector General for the LAPD) to monitor the internal disciplinary process of police departments. This has reportedly been effective in identifying systemic weaknesses and serving to improve the quality of investigations.

Federal government

The Justice Department may bring federal criminal civil rights charges against state or federal officials who violate the rights of others while acting under "color of law". However, of the thousands of complaints filed with the Justice Department each year, only a small proportion result in prosecutions.[70] This is partly because the federal rules of evidence in such cases are particularly stringent, with a requirement to

---

[68] For example, the Independent Counsel for Albuquerque was criticized for issuing minimal reports (Luna and Walker, op.cit.) and Amnesty International was told in 1997 that the Office of Special Investigations of the Chicago PD issued no data by type of complaint or race.

[69] The Civilian Review Board in Atlanta, Georgia, had such limited powers and low visibility that the Mayor of Atlanta did not even know of its existence, according to a 1996 Human Rights Watch report (*Modern Capital of Human Rights? Abuses in the State of Georgia*, July 1996). The Civilian Review Board in Baltimore, Maryland, had a similarly low profile and limited review function, according to information given to Amnesty International in November 1997.

[70] During a meeting with staff of the Justice Department's Civil Rights Division in November 1997, Amnesty International was told that the criminal division had received 11,000 civil rights complaints from October 1996 to September 1997. Although the majority involved misconduct by officials, they also covered other issues including "hate crimes" such as racially motivated church arson. During the same period the division had prosecuted 77 cases, involving 189 defendants, approximately a third of whom were law enforcement officials.

© AI

Many instances of police abusing their power only come to light through the
determined and tireless work of human rights campaigners, civil rights
lawyers and relatives of the victims.

prove beyond reasonable doubt that the official in question acted with
specific intent to violate a protected right.

Until 1994, the Justice Department was limited to pursuing individual criminal prosecutions, but it lacked the power to investigate
broader problems within police departments. However, the Police
Accountability Act, incorporated into the Violent Crime Control and
Law Enforcement Act of 1994 (Crime Control Act), gave the Justice
Department the authority to bring civil actions in federal courts against
police departments accused of engaging in a "pattern or practice" of
abuses. This is an important new remedy which has led to a significant
reform program being drawn up in at least one police department: the
Consent Decree formulated as a result of the federal investigation into
the Pittsburgh Police Bureau. While this could serve as a model for
other police agencies, by mid-1998, the Justice Department had brought
a similar action against only one other department — the Steubenville
Police Department in Ohio — although investigations into several other
agencies were pending. However, the Justice Department does not have

the resources to investigate more than a small proportion of problem agencies. The section which handles such cases has seen its brief expand considerably without a commensurate increase in staff.

Most police agencies receive federal grants to support aspects of their work. Title VI of the Civil Rights Act, 1964, prohibits discrimination on grounds of race, colour, national origin, sex or religion by state and local law enforcement agencies, and allows the Justice Department to withhold grants or make them conditional on compliance. This statute has been used most often in relation to hiring and training policies; at the time of writing the Civil Rights Division was reportedly considering its use against racially biased practices such as traffic stops.

Lack of national data

Monitoring of police conduct in the USA is hampered by the lack of accurate, comprehensive national data on police use of force, including the numbers of people killed or injured through police shootings or other types of force. Although many police departments require officers to report all serious use-of-force incidents, few state governments keep state-wide records. Those that do depend largely on self-reporting by the agencies concerned.

Civil rights organizations have long pressed for national monitoring and reporting on police use of force, to enable the federal government to identify patterns of concern. A national reporting system was mandated by Congress when it passed the Crime Control Act of 1994, which directed the US Attorney General to acquire data about the use of excessive force by law enforcement officers for research and statistical purposes and to publish an annual summary. However, Congress, while passing the legislation, has not yet provided funds to do the work.[71]

Recommendations

Federal, state and local authorities should take immediate action to halt human rights violations by police officers. They should make clear that

---

[71] Two pilot projects were set up in 1995 and 1996: one to develop a model for collecting data from local police agencies, and the other to design a national survey of the public on police-public contacts. A Justice Department report on the results of the pilot project states: "Because funding was specifically requested to fulfil the Title XXI mandate for annual data collection on the police use of excessive force, but was not provided, it is unclear whether the pilot efforts can be continued." (Bureau of Justice Statistics report: *Police Use of Force, Collection of National Data*, November 1997) At the time of writing, the projects were on hold, pending requests for further funding.

abuses including torture, brutality and other excessive force by police officers will not be tolerated; that officers will be held accountable for their actions; and that those responsible for abuses will be brought to justice. Victims of abuse by police officers should be guaranteed effective and timely reparation. International human rights standards should be fully incorporated into police codes of conduct and training.

1. The administration should seek, and Congress should provide, adequate funding to enable the Justice Department to fulfill its mandate under the Police Accountability Act provisions of the Violent Crime Control and Law Enforcement Act of 1994. The Special Litigation Section should be enabled to fulfill its task of pursuing "pattern and practice"lawsuits against police agencies nationwide which commit wide-spread abuses. The Justice Department should compile and regularly publish detailed national data on police use of force (including all police fatal shootings and deaths in custody), withanalysis of patterns of concern and policy recommendations.

2. The federal government should increase its use of Title VI of the Civil Rights Act of 1964 to seek to eliminate racially discriminatory treatment by law enforcement agencies. Funding should be contingent upon agencies which engage in discriminatory practices taking effective steps to eliminate them.

3. All allegations of human rights violations and other police misconduct should be fully and impartially investigated, in line with best practice for such investigations. All officers responsible for abuses should be adequately disciplined, and, where appropriate, prosecuted.

4. There should be greater transparency in the investigation of complaints of human rights violations. Complainants should be kept informed of the progress of these investigations. The outcome of all criminal, disciplinary and administrative investigations into alleged violations, and into all disputed shootings and deaths in police custody, should be made public promptly after the completion of the investigation.

5. Police departments should provide information on the internal disciplinary process by publishing regular statistical data on the type and outcome of complaints and disciplinary action. They should also publish regular statistics on the number of people shot and killed or injured by police officers and other deaths in custody.

6. City and county authorities should be required to forward information on civil lawsuits alleging police misconduct to the police department and to relevant oversight bodies. They should regularly make public information on the number of lawsuits filed, and judgments and settlements.

7. Police departments should ensure that their policies on the use of force and firearms conform to international standards. All police departments should ban hogtying and choke holds.

8. The federal authorities should establish an independent review of the use of OC (pepper) spray by law enforcement agencies. Police departments which continue to authorize the spray should introduce strict guidelines and limitations on its use, with clear monitoring procedures.

9. Law enforcement and correctional agencies should suspend the use of electro-shock weapons such as stun guns and tasers pending the outcome of a rigorous, independent and impartial inquiry into the use and effects of the equipment.

10. Federal, state and local authorities, including police departments, should ensure that training programs include: international standards on human rights, particularly the prohibition on torture and ill-treatment; how to deal with situations which have often led to excessive force, including pursuits and how to cope with disturbed individuals; gender issues; and sensitivity to minority groups.

11. Police departments should establish early warning systems to identify and deal with officers involved in human rights violations. They should establish clear reporting systems and keep detailed records of every officer's conduct. They should conduct regular audits of these records in order to identify, and take remedial action in respect of, any patterns of abuse, including racial bias or other discriminatory treatment. These audits should be open to inspection or view by independent oversight bodies.

12. Police departments should issue clear guidelines requiring officers to report abuses, and officers with chain-of-command control should be held responsible for enforcing those guidelines and strictly enforcing penalties for failing to report, or covering up, abuses.

13. State, local and federal authorities should establish independent and effective oversight bodies for their respective police agencies. In particular, these bodies should:

— have the authority to investigate or review complaints of human rights violations by the public against the police;

— be able to conduct regular audits of the police internal complaints and disciplinary process and, where necessary, conduct their own investigations;

— have the power to require witnesses to appear and to insist on cooperation from police departments and individual officers;

— require police agencies to provide information on action taken in individual cases, with reasons for inaction;

— have the authority to review and make recommendations on policy and training;

— provide detailed public reports, at least annually, giving relevant data, including the type of complaint and the race and gender of the complainant and the accused officer.

— publicize the complaints procedure within the community and ensure that it is accessible to the public; information about complaints procedures should be prominently displayed in all police stations.

4

VIOLATIONS IN PRISONS AND JAILS: Needless brutality

"A pattern of needless and officially sanctioned brutality."

This was how the treatment of prisoners in Pelican Bay State Prison, California, was described by a federal court in 1995. The abuses included severe beatings during the forcible removal of prisoners from cells, the cruel use of shackles, and the unwarranted use of firearms. The judge found that the guards were rarely disciplined for excessive force and covered up abuses with false or inadequate reports.[1]

Every day in prisons and jails across the USA, the human rights of prisoners are violated. In many facilities, violence is endemic. In some cases, guards fail to stop inmates assaulting each other. In others, the guards are themselves the abusers, subjecting their victims to beatings and sexual abuse. Prisons and jails use mechanical, chemical and electro-shock methods of restraint that are cruel, degrading and sometimes life-threatening. The victims of abuse include pregnant women and the mentally ill.

Thousands of prisoners are isolated in solitary confinement for long periods. Many prisoners do not receive adequate care for serious physical and mental health problems.

Many of these practices violate US laws as well as international human rights standards[2], but the mechanisms available to prevent abuses and provide redress are inadequate. The weakness of independent scrutiny, together with public demands for harsher treatment of offenders, have created a climate in which serious violations can occur and continue without being effectively challenged.

[1] *Madrid v. Gomez*, 889 F. Supp. 1146.1255 (N.D. Cal 1995). As a result of the lawsuit the prison authorities have been required to implement a series of policy changes covering use of force, investigations and discipline, medical and mental health care.

[2] In particular, the ICCPR, the Convention against Torture, the Standard Minimum Rules for the Treatment of Prisoners, and the Body of Principles for the Protection of All Persons under Any Form of Detention or Imprisonment.

A system under pressure

In mid-1997 there were over 1.7 million people incarcerated in US jails and prisons, more than three times the 1980 figure. The increase reflected long-term rises in crime, and state and federal sentencing policies which have led to longer prison terms, fewer releases on parole, and mandatory minimum prison sentences, especially for drugs offences.

Over 60 per cent of prisoners are from racial and ethnic minority backgrounds. Half are African Americans, even though they comprise just over 12 per cent of the US population. The proportion of prisoners from minority groups has been growing steadily. One reason for this has been the disproportionate impact of drug sentencing policies on black Americans. Between 1985 and 1995 drugs offences accounted for 42 per cent of the increase in the number of blacks jailed, compared to 26 per cent for whites.[3]

There has also been a higher rate of increase in women prisoners than men: women now comprise over 10 per cent of the jail population and over six per cent of the prison population. In 1970 there were about 5,600 women in state and federal prisons; by 1997 there were 75,000.[4] The increase is due in large part to a massive rise in the number of women incarcerated for drugs offences.[5]

Even though huge sums have been spent on building new prisons and jails in the past decade, the expansion has not kept pace with the rising prison population. Overcrowding and understaffing have contributed to dangerous and inhumane conditions in many facilities. The Justice Department and others have documented appalling conditions in dozens of jails: overflowing toilets and pipes; toxic and insanitary environments; prisoners forced to sleep on filthy floors without mattresses; cells infested with vermin and lacking ventilation.[6] Some of the

---

[3] Bureau of Justice Statistics Bulletin, June 1997.

[4] The 1970 figure is from E. Currie, *Crime and Punishment in America*, Metropolitan Books, New York, 1998; the 1997 figure is from D. Gilliard and A. Beck, "Prison and jail inmates at midyear 1997", *Bureau of Justice Statistics Bulletin*, January 1998.

[5] Between 1986 and 1991, the number of women serving sentences for drugs offences increased by 432 per cent, according to Justice Department figures.

[6] A Justice Department investigation into 18 Mississippi jails in 1993 found hazardous and squalid conditions in many facilities, including overcrowding, insufficient staffing, grossly deficient medical care and inadequate suicide prevention measures. Four jails were ordered to be closed. The Justice Department has since made similar findings in jails in other states, including Virginia and Georgia.

Prisoners during a mass search in Ellis 1 Unit, Huntsville, Texas

jails investigated by the Justice Department were found not to have any policies or procedures on the use of force.[7] In others policies or training were inadequate.

Overcrowded correctional facilities lack the space and staff to protect vulnerable inmates from predatory ones. As a result, physical and sexual violence and extortion are rife in many prisons and jails. In the Yavapai County jail system in Arizona, for instance, particularly in Prescott Jail, beatings by inmates were allegedly a daily occurrence in 1997.[8] Violence between prisoners is aggravated by confining inmates together who should be separated. For example, in Nebraska State

[7] For example, the Findings Letter on Orleans County Jail, New York, dated January 1998, reported that the authors were unable to identify any use of force policy or procedure at the jail or any training on the use of force. Similar findings have been made in other facilities.

[8] As reported to Amnesty International during a visit to Arizona in June 1997.

Prison, overcrowding led to prisoners being confined together without any review of their backgrounds, reportedly leading to an increase in assaults, rapes and robberies by inmates.[9] Rape of prisoners by other inmates is reported to be alarmingly widespread. In a 1994 survey of prisoners in Nebraska, more than 10 per cent of male prisoners reported being "pressured or forced to have sexual contact" with other inmates.[10]

Contrary to international standards, some jails do not segregate pre-trial detainees from convicted prisoners.[11] There is often little or no classification of people who may be awaiting trial for minor or serious crimes, and inmates are commonly housed together in dormitories.[12] For example, in the second half of 1997 Los Angeles County Jail continued to house inmates in unsuitable dormitories, even though many were awaiting trial on dangerous felony charges. Inmates were reported to have preyed on the mentally ill, stealing their food and possessions and attacking them.[13]

The increase in the prison population has coincided with a shift away from rehabilitation towards greater emphasis on incapacitation and punishment. This has often led to the imposition of harsher regimes and cuts in amenities. Despite evidence that education can reduce reoffending rates, educational programs have been cut, and in 1994 Congress ended all provision of federal funds for prisoners participating in higher education.[14] In many facilities exercise equipment has been removed and leisure activities severely restricted.

---

[9] *Prison Legal News*, December 1996, reporting on an ongoing lawsuit.

[10] C. Struckman-Johnson et al, "Sexual Coercion Reported by Men and Women in Prison", The Journal of Sex Research, vol.33, No.1, 1996. See also, J. Gilligan, *Violence — reflections on a national epidemic*, Vintage Books, New York, 1997.

[11] ICCPR Article 10(2); Rules 8 and 85.1 of the Standard Minimum Rules; Principle 8 of the Body of Principles.

[12] The Standard Minimum Rules provide that prisoners should be kept apart, taking account of factors such as their criminal record (Rule 8), and that dormitories should be occupied by prisoners carefully selected as being suitable to associate with each other, and be regularly supervised at night (Rule 9(2)).

[13] Justice Department CRIPA investigation of Mental Health Services in the Los Angeles County Jail, September 1997.

[14] "Education as crime prevention — providing education to prisoners", Occasional Paper, Series No.2, The Center on Crime, Communities and Culture, New York, September 1997. At least 25 states have reportedly reduced vocational and technical training for prisoners, and the number of higher education programs fell from 350 in 1990 to 8 in 1997.

The pressure faced by correctional staff in coping with overcrowding and poorly equipped facilities has led to an increased use of mechanical and other forms of control in some institutions. A wide range of technology designed to control and incapacitate inmates has been developed in recent years, including electro-shock devices, which Amnesty International believes are inherently unsafe and prone to misuse. The growth of supermaximum security units to house large numbers of prisoners in isolation for extended periods is also part of the shift towards containment and punishment instead of rehabilitation.

In order to cut costs, states have increasingly contracted out to private firms the management of facilities as well as services such as health care. As a result, incarceration has become one of the fastest growing businesses in the USA, generating large profits for the corporations that now house more than 77,000 prison and jail inmates.[15] Many experts believe that the involvement of private companies increases the likelihood of inmates being abused and subjected to poor conditions. They suggest that private companies have a stronger interest in cutting costs, which can lead to low investment in staffing, training, health care, educational or rehabilitation programs, and even food. Such fears are borne out by serious complaints about conditions in privately run facilities in a number of states.

As local facilities have run out of room, a growing number of states have transported prisoners to out-of-state facilities, often thousands of miles away. For example, women prisoners from Hawaii, many of whom had young children, were transferred to a former jail — now a privately run prison — in Crystal City, Texas. Hundreds of Alaskan prisoners have been sent to private prisons in Arizona. Such transferrals can cause extreme hardship, including loss of contact with family and friends, and problems in communicating with lawyers.[16]

Standards for protecting prisoners

International treaties, as well as US national and state civil and criminal laws, clearly spell out safeguards to protect the physical and mental well-being of those deprived of their liberty. Under the ICCPR and the

---

[15] Eric Bates, "Private Prisons", *The Nation*, 5 January 1998. This figure does not include private juvenile detention and correctional facilities, or facilities for undocumented immigrants and asylum-seekers, which house thousands.

[16] The importance of maintaining links with family and community is recognized in the Standard Minimum Rules (Rules 80 and 92) and Principles 18 and 20 of the Body of Principles.

Convention against Torture, the US government is obliged to ensure that people are not subjected to torture (including rape) or to cruel, inhuman or degrading treatment[17], and that people deprived of their liberty are treated with humanity and with respect for the dignity of the human person[18].

When it ratified the ICCPR (in 1992) and the Convention against Torture (in 1994), the USA sought to limit the obligations imposed by the treaties. For example, it declared that the ICCPR's prohibition on torture and cruel, inhuman or degrading treatment would apply only to the narrower "cruel and unusual punishment", which is prohibited by the US Constitution.

The Supreme Court and lower courts have interpreted the prohibition on cruel and unusual punishment and other provisions of the Constitution as providing people in prisons and jails with a range of rights in areas such as physical safety, medical care, access to the courts and procedural safeguards in disciplinary hearings. There are also state laws that provide rights to inmates because they apply to everyone (such as laws against assault) or to prisoners specifically (such as laws prohibiting sexual relations between correctional staff and inmates). However, in many areas, such as the use of restraints, the supervision of women prisoners and the separation of children from adults, US law provides a lower level of protection than international standards.

National professional bodies, in particular the American Correctional Association (ACA) and the National Commission on Correctional Health Care (NCCHC), have developed detailed standards for prisons and jails, some of which cover matters that are the subject of human rights standards. Both bodies operate voluntary accreditation programs, and their standards are binding only on those states or institutions which opt to join. Not all prisons are accredited (60 per cent are accredited by the ACA and 25 per cent by the NCCHC), and only a small proportion of jails are accredited (4 per cent by the ACA and 7 per cent by the NCCHC).

Physical brutality

Abuses by correctional staff using excessive or unnecessary force include the following:

- individual cases of excessive force and assaults by guards;
- widespread, systematic abuse in particular institutions;
- organized ill-treatment by guards as punishment, including attacks on unresisting prisoners;

---

[17] Article 7 of the ICCPR.
[18] Article 10 of the ICCPR.

- guards inciting or permitting inmates to attack other inmates.

The following cases illustrate a range of concerns in some of the largest state correctional systems.

Georgia: In July 1996, 14 inmates were injured following beatings during a "shakedown" (a mass search for contraband items) at Hays State Prison. The head of the corrections department allegedly supervised the beatings of scores of handcuffed prisoners by a prison tactical squad (a special riot squad) during shakedowns in several state prisons in 1996.[19] Court cases alleging ill-treatment during shakedowns in at least two other Georgia prisons were pending in mid-1998.

California: Guards at Corcoran State Prison are alleged to have deliberately staged "gladiator" fights between inmates and placed bets on the outcome. Between 1988 and 1994, seven prisoners were shot dead and dozens of others wounded when armed guards fired on them. Lawyers acting for relatives of victims obtained prison videotapes that contradicted official accounts of the shootings. Two prison guards who gave evidence to a subsequent FBI investigation were reportedly harassed by their fellow officers and eventually forced to resign.

New York: In October 1996, 11 correctional officers were charged with having planned concerted attacks on inmates in the punitive segregation unit of Rikers Island Penal Complex in New York City, and with filing false reports to cover up the abuses. By May 1998, two had been sentenced to prison terms. The authorities had reportedly been alerted to an unusual number of injuries sustained by prisoners in the unit soon after it opened in 1988, but internal inquiries failed to establish guard misconduct. The abuses were exposed when the Legal Aid Society[20] filed a civil lawsuit in 1993. In 1996 the city paid $1.6 million to 15 individuals who had been beaten in the unit between 1990 and 1992. However, Legal Aid Service lawyers were still receiving allegations of abuse in late 1997 from inmates in a new segregation unit at the jail.

Pennsylvania: In November 1997 an Amnesty International delegation visiting SCI-Greene, a supermaximum prison housing the state's death

---

[19] Although the prison authorities continue to deny wrongdoing, in February 1998 inmates received $283,000 damages in settlement of a civil lawsuit. Claims that the head of the corrections department had watched the Hays Prison beatings were supported in pre-trial witness statements by several prison employees. The lawsuit was brought by the Southern Center for Human Rights, a Georgia-based non-profit organization of attorneys who represent indigent prisoners in several southern states.

[20] The Legal Aid Society is a non-profit organization which provides free legal services to the poor.

row population, received information that prisoners, most of them black, were being beaten by guards and subjected to racist taunts and false disciplinary charges. In May 1998, following an internal investigation, several guards were dismissed and some 20 others disciplined for abuses against inmates in the prison's disciplinary segregation unit.

Texas: Two guards who beat a prisoner to death in Terrell Unit in 1994 were released on parole after serving only a few months in prison. They had been sentenced to eight and 10 years' imprisonment respectively. In August 1997 a videotape, apparently compiled for training purposes, showed guards in a privately run section of Brazoria County Detention Center, Texas, kicking and beating inmates, coaxing dogs to bite prisoners and using stun guns.

Arizona: Following a disturbance in Graham Unit, Arizona State Prison, in August 1995, more than 600 prisoners were forced by guards to remain handcuffed outdoors for 96 hours, and to defecate and urinate in their clothes. During daylight hours the heat was intense and many suffered serious sunburn, heat exhaustion and dehydration.

Sexual abuse

In 1997 the Justice Department sued the states of Michigan and Arizona, alleging that they were failing to protect women from sexual misconduct, including sexual assaults and "prurient viewing during dressing, showering and use of toilet facilities".[21] In 1998 the Federal Bureau of Prisons agreed to pay three women $500,000 to settle a lawsuit in which the women claimed that they had been beaten, raped and sold by guards for sex with male inmates at a federal correctional facility in California.[22] Such cases highlight the increasing number of reports of sexual abuse committed by correctional staff against inmates in jails and prisons around the country.[23]

Reported sexual abuses by correctional staff include rape and other coerced sexual acts; staff routinely subjecting inmates to sexually offensive language; staff deliberately touching intimate parts of inmates' bodies during searches; and staff watching inmates who are undressed.

Rape of inmates by prison officials is a form of torture.[24] Rape and

[21] *US v. Arizona*, CIV 97 - 476 PHX ROS; *US v. Michigan*, Case No. 97-4005.

[22] *Lucas v. White*, C96-2905.

[23] See Human Rights Watch, *All too familiar — sexual abuse of women in US state prisons*, New York, 1996.

[24] See UN Commission on Human Rights, UN Doc. E/CN.4/1995/34, January 1995, para.189.

© Donna Binder/Impact Visuals

In Alabama prisoners have been tied to a restraint pole (known as the "hitching rail") as punishment, sometimes for hours in sweltering heat or freezing conditions. At Julia Tutwiler Prison for Women in Alabama, inmates have been handcuffed to the rail for up to a day. In January 1997 a federal magistrate ruled that the state should stop using the rail, describing it as a "painful and tortuous punishment". However, a state appeal against the ruling was still pending in July 1998.

other coerced sexual acts violate basic international human rights standards such as the Convention against Torture as well as national and state laws and staff codes of conduct. One reason for the prevalence of rape and sexual abuse is that victims are afraid to complain. As the Justice Department stated following its investigation of prisons in Michigan, "Many sexual relationships appear to be unreported due to the presently widespread fear of retaliation and vulnerability felt by these women".[25]

There are legal and disciplinary sanctions against sexual abuse in prisons and jails. Thirty-five states, the District of Colombia and the federal government have laws specifically making sexual abuse in prisons a criminal offence. In 13 states, it is an offence for staff to have sexual

---

[25] Justice Department, letter to Governor of Michigan, 27 March 1995.

relations with inmates.[26] The National Institute of Corrections (part of the Justice Department) provides training and advice to correctional authorities on the prevention of sexual misconduct in women's prisons, and a number of states and the Federal Bureau of Prisons have introduced special measures to stop abuse and to handle complaints. However, at the time of writing, eight states still had no laws criminalizing sexual relations between staff and inmates in prisons: Alabama, Kentucky, Massachusetts, Minnesota, Montana, Virginia, Washington and West Virginia.

Complaints about coerced sex and sexually offensive language have usually been made by female inmates about male staff. However, there have also been reports of sexual coercion by female staff against both male and female inmates, and by male staff against male inmates.[27] Both male and female inmates have complained about intimate body searches and surveillance by staff of the opposite sex. The main underlying source of such complaints is that US correctional facilities employ both men and women to supervise prisoners of the opposite sex, allow them to undertake searches involving body contact, and permit them to be present where inmates are naked. The employment of male staff to supervise female inmates breaches international standards, which provide that male staff must not enter part of a prison set aside for women unless accompanied by a female officer and that women prisoners must be attended and supervised only by women officers.[28]

US courts have ruled that anti-discrimination laws mean that correctional facilities cannot refuse to employ men in female facilities or women in male facilities. The (UN) Human Rights Committee[29] has expressed concern at the practice "which has led to serious allegations of sexual abuse of women and the invasion of their privacy". It called on the US authorities to amend existing legislation "so as to provide at least that they [male officers] will always be accompanied by women officers."[30] The UN Body of Principles for the Protection of All Persons under Any Form of Detention or Imprisonment states that "measures applied under the law and designed

---

[26] B. Smith, *Fifty-state survey of criminal laws prohibiting sexual abuse of prisoners*, National Women's Law Center, Washington DC, 1998.

[27] See, for example, C. Struckman-Johnson, op. cit.

[28] Rule 53 of the Standard Minimum Rules.

[29] The Human Rights Committee is a body of experts which monitors compliance with the ICCPR.

[30] Comments of Human Rights Committee on the report submitted by the USA concerning its compliance with the ICCPR, UN Doc. CCPR/C/79/Add.50, 7 April 1995, paras 20 and 34.

solely to protect the rights and status of women...shall not be deemed to be discriminatory". Amnesty International believes that the nature and extent of sexual abuse in US prisons and jails require strict compliance with the international standard that female inmates should be attended by female staff.

Abusive use of restraints

The cruel use of restraints, resulting in unnecessary pain, injury or even death, is widespread in US prisons and jails. Mentally disturbed prisoners have been bound, spread-eagled, on boards for prolonged periods in four-point restraints without proper medical authorization or supervision. Restraints are deliberately imposed as punishment, or used as a routine control measure rather than as an emergency response. Such practices breach international standards.[31]

US correctional and health professional standards provide safeguards, including checks on restraints at 15-minute intervals by health professionals or health-care trained staff; time limits on the use of restraints; medical authorization of restraints for mental health or medical purposes; and the use of soft rather than metal restraints for "therapeutic" purposes.[32] However, these guidelines are voluntary. There are no nationally binding minimum standards regarding the use of restraints, and policies, practices and monitoring systems vary widely.

US law does not bar the use of chains or leg-irons, even though their use as restraints is expressly prohibited by international standards. It is common practice for prisoners and detainees to be shackled during transportation, with handcuffs attached to metal waist chains and, in many cases, the legs or ankles chained together.

[31] The Standard Minimum Rules stipulate that: "Instruments of restraint, such as handcuffs, chains, irons and strait-jackets, shall never be applied as a punishment. Furthermore, chains or irons shall not be used as restraints". They further provide that restraints may only be used when other measures are ineffective and only for so long as is "strictly necessary". (Rules 31, 33 and 34)

[32] The ACA states that "Four-point restraints should be used only in extreme instances and only when other types of restraints have proven to be ineffective", with 15-minute observation checks. The American Public Health Association (APHA) and the NCCHC provide that restraints for medical or mental health purposes should be imposed only on the order of a qualified health professional, and only if no other less restrictive treatment is appropriate. The NCCHC recommends that the use of therapeutic restraints should generally not exceed 12 hours; APHA provides for automatic termination after four hours, renewable for a maximum of four more hours. The NCCHC 1997 standards expressly state that, "Persons should not be restrained in an unnatural position (for instance, hog-tied, face-down, spread-eagle)".

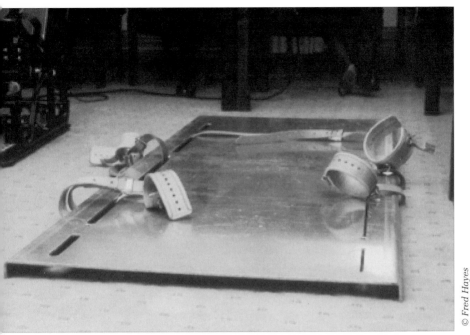

© Fred Hayes

In Utah State Prison an inmate with a history of self-mutilation was shackled to a steel board on a cell floor in four-point metal restraints for 12 weeks in 1995. He was removed from the board on average four times a week to shower. At other times he was left to defecate while lying on the board. He was released from the board only following a court order.

Prolonged immobilization in restraints carries a risk of potentially fatal blood clots and certain positions can lead to positional asphyxia. There are other risks. For example, a prisoner at the Halawa Correctional Facility, Hawaii, was treated for more than 20 open sores and ulcers after being held for two weeks in a bare cell in wrist-to-waist metal shackles and leg-irons as punishment in 1995. Two years earlier a man had his right leg amputated after he was strapped to a bed for eight days in Los Angeles County Jail. At least two other inmates in the same jail had earlier died from blood clots as a result of prolonged immobilization in restraints. Although the jail has since improved its procedures, the death of a female inmate in 1996, possibly connected to the use of restraints, was reported in 1997.[33]

---

[33] Findings Letter of Justice Department on mental health services in the jail, 15 November 1997, cites the death of a woman which "may have been related to the jail's use of restraints".

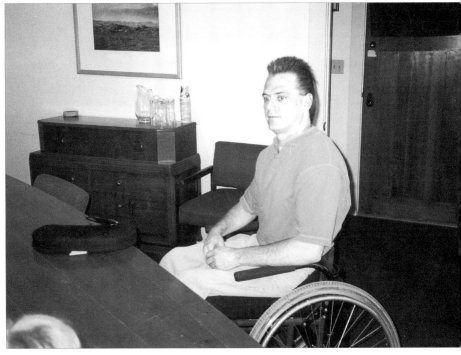

© AI

Richard Post, a paraplegic, was admitted to Madison Street Jail, Phoenix, Arizona, in March 1996. Detention officers removed him from his wheelchair and strapped him into a four-point restraint chair, with his arms pulled down towards his ankles and padlocked, and his legs secured in metal shackles. He developed severe ulcers and the tightness of the restraints reportedly damaged his spinal cord, resulting in significant loss of upper body mobility.

The restraint chair

Some of the most serious abuses in recent years have involved a steel-framed restraint chair which allows a prisoner to be immobilized with four-point restraints securing both arms and legs, and straps which can be tightened across the shoulders and chest. The chair has been promoted as a safer alternative to other forms of four-point restraint as the prisoner remains in an upright sitting position. This has not, however, prevented prisoners from being tortured or ill-treated while strapped in the chair. Most of the reported abuses have taken place in jails, particularly in the intake (reception) areas, which are often acutely overcrowded and handle people shortly after arrest, when they may be agitated or intoxicated.[34] The initial decision to place people in the chair is often taken by guards without appropriate medical evaluation. In some institutions the chair appears to be used as a routine method of control rather than as a crisis measure. The chair also appears to have been used as punishment for mildly challenging behaviour. The following cases illustrate some of these concerns.

Iberia Parish Jail, Louisiana: A lawsuit filed by the Justice Department in 1996 claimed that sheriff's deputies had routinely subjected inmates to "cruel and unusual punishment, and physical and mental torture" by leaving them strapped in restraint chairs for extended periods in their own urine and excrement. According to the lawsuit, prisoners in the chair had their feet strapped behind them and their hands shackled behind or beneath their buttocks. Some prisoners had tape wrapped round their mouths and football helmets placed backwards on their heads. They were, "rarely, if ever, examined by medical personnel while restrained or after release". One 18-year-old inmate was reportedly held in the chair for eight days, another inmate for 43 hours.[35] The jail authorities agreed to stop using the chair and hogtying (restraining with the ankles bound from behind to the wrists) inmates as part of a pre-trial settlement in December 1996.

Utah State Prison: Michael Valent died as a result of a blood clot in March 1997 after being held for 16 hours in a restraint chair. His feet were secured with metal shackles and the seat had a hole to allow him to defecate and urinate without moving. The prison authorities reported in April 1997 that they had used the chair more than 200 times to restrain prisoners, most of whom were mentally ill, for up to five days since it had been introduced in late 1995. The state's mental health department told Amnesty International in July 1997 that the Department of Corrections had stopped using the restraint chair.

Madison Street Jail, Maricopa County, Arizona: In June 1996 Scott Norberg died of asphyxia after being placed in a restraint chair with a towel wrapped over his face after he refused to leave his cell; before being strapped in the chair he was hit more than 20 times with an

---

[34] The chair is marketed under the trade name "Prostraint" by AEDEC International Inc, a company based in Oregon. The president of AEDEC International was unable to provide Amnesty International with information on the number of facilities which had purchased restraint chairs, but stated that they were in use in more jails than state prisons, as the procedures for adopting them in jails were easier. (Interview, October 1997)

[35] *Times Picayune*, 3 December 1996.

Members of the Maricopa County Jail's all-female "chain gang" carrying a coffin to its burial place, Phoenix, Arizona.

© Stan Grossfeld/Boston Globe

69

electric stun gun. The chair remains in use in the jail. In 1997 officials told a visiting Amnesty International delegation that the jail system had 16 chairs which had been used about 600 times in six months.[36]

St Lucie County Jail, Florida: In December 1996 Anderson Tate, who had swallowed cocaine when arrested, died while strapped in a restraint chair. He was in the chair for three hours, moaning and chanting prayers, while jailers taunted him and ignored his pleas for help. Two deputies were dismissed after an administrative investigation by the Sheriff's Department, but no criminal charges were filed.

Sacramento County Jail, California: At least nine people alleged that they were tortured or ill-treated in 1996 by being placed in restraint chairs. Three said that deputies had told them they were about to be electrocuted when they were put in the chair; the two deputies were later suspended for 15 days. One woman was allegedly hooded and strapped into the chair as punishment after guards overheard her complain about her treatment; another suffered skin injuries through being held in tight straps for a prolonged period.

Pregnant women shackled

Many women are pregnant when they are imprisoned. In 1996 more than 1,000 babies were born to women in US prisons. Because few prisons and jails have childbirth facilities, almost all are transported to hospitals to give birth and for antenatal visits. They are usually held in some form of mechanical restraint when being transported and sometimes in hospital. A court in Washington DC condemned as "inhumane" the practice of shackling women in labour and shortly after. It heard evidence of one woman who was placed in handcuffs and leg shackles when "she had not yet purged the afterbirth".[37]

Prisoners in Connecticut and California have reported being shackled in full restraints while they were pregnant: "Pregnant women who are shackled at their wrists, ankles and waists are more likely to fall, and more likely to injure themselves and their foetuses because they cannot use their hands to protect their bodies".[38]

---

[36] See Amnesty International, *USA: Ill-treatment of inmates in Maricopa County Jails, Arizona*, August 1997 (AI Index: AMR 51/51/97).

[37] *Women Prisoners of the District of Columbia Department of Corrections v. DC*, Civil Action No. 93-2052, 877 F. Supp.634.

[38] L.Acoca, "Defusing the time bomb: understanding and meeting the growing health care needs of incarcerated women in America", *Crime and Delinquency*, Vol 44 No.1, January 1998.

© AP/Christopher Berkey

Rescue workers remove the charred bodies of six prison inmates from a transport van that caught fire in Tennessee in April 1997. The driver and guard were not able to save the state prisoners, who were chained and shackled.

Gas and chemical sprays

Scores of prisoners transferred from Washington DC to a private prison in Ohio experienced chest and respiratory problems after guards dropped up to 20 canisters of tear-gas into their cell blocks without warning, following a small non-violent protest. The incident happened in the Northeast Ohio Correctional Center in May 1997. The victims were reportedly given no medical treatment or opportunity to shower. Soon afterwards, some were allegedly sprayed directly in the face with mace as a punishment while handcuffed; some were subjected to racial taunts by guards. According to testimony, prisoners were only allowed to wash the mace off their faces after several hours, by which time many had peeling skin.[39]

Many other complaints on behalf of prisoners from around the country have reported inmates suffering unwarranted exposure to

---

[39] Testimony of Jonathan M. Smith, Executive Director of DC Prisoners' Legal Services Project, 27 August 1997. The prison is run by the Corrections Corporation of America (CCA), the largest private prison company in the USA.

chemical sprays, such as having pepper (OC) spray, mace or tear-gas sprayed directly into their faces, or from excessive spraying in enclosed spaces. Sammy Marshall, a mentally ill prisoner in San Quentin Prison, California, died in June 1997 after guards repeatedly used OC spray for more than an hour when he barricaded himself into his cell. The coroner found that the most likely cause of death was an allergic reaction to OC spray. In 1997 Oklahoma took back inmates from Limestone County Detention Facility in Texas following concern at the extensive use by guards of OC spray.[40]

A report on Los Angeles County Jail found that the use of OC spray (and other force) had increased dramatically in the jail's reception building between 1994 and 1995. The report observed that OC spray was best deployed outdoors rather than inside a jail where it could be "as noxious to the deputies deploying it and to bystanders as to the target inmates". The report also noted that some deputies believed that their training was inadequate. One stated "The new deputies don't know how to physically restrain inmates. All they know is to use the spray."[41]

Electro-shock devices

Electro-shock weapons, including stun belts, stun shields and stun guns, are also used in US prisons. Amnesty International believes that such devices are inherently subject to, and even invite, abuse. In the Maricopa County jail system, for example, stun guns have allegedly been used to inflict repeated shocks on inmates, including on those already restrained. In one instance, a stun gun was used to arouse an inmate from sleep.[42]

A Justice Department report into a Kentucky jail in April 1998 found that: "staff misuse and abuse weapons such as pepper spray, stun shields, and stun guns, resorting to them early and often, for both management and punishment." The report cites a case in which a guard used a stun gun to rouse an inmate who had "passed out".[43]

In 1996 in Muncy Prison, Pennsylvania, staff used an "Electronic

[40] *New York Times*, 21 August 1997.

[41] 6th Semiannual report by Special Counsel Merrick J. Bobb and Staff, September 1996.

[42] See Amnesty International, August 1997, op. cit, and Findings Letter of Justice Department to the Maricopa County Board of Supervisors, dated 25 March 1996.

[43] Letter from Justice Department to County Court Judge on the Daviess County Detention Center, Kentucky, 10 April 1998.

Body Immobilizer Device" to subdue a woman prisoner who was in great distress after a warrant for her execution had been read. According to Amnesty International's information she posed no threat to anyone else, and the organization expressed concern about the case to the Department of Corrections. Officials confirmed that the device was used to gain control of the woman, "who was perpetrating significant self-injurious behavior and was unresponsive to the directions given to her by the supervising commissioned officer" and stated that the use of the device in these circumstances "conformed to Department policy".[44]

Companies that market such weapons claim they are safe and non-lethal if used properly. Other experts warn that electro-shock weapons can be harmful, even lethal, for people with high blood pressure, for pregnant women, and for those suffering epilepsy and some other conditions. In light of this, stun weapons have been banned for law enforcement use by a number of countries, including Canada and most West European countries, as well as some US states.

The introduction of remote control electro-shock stun belts for use on US prisoners is of particular concern. The belt, which a guard can activate by the push of a button, inflicts a powerful electric current, causing severe pain and instant incapacitation. According to the manufacturer's literature, the activated belt will knock the prisoner to the ground and may cause him or her to defecate or urinate.

The belt is used by the US Bureau of Prisons, the US Marshall's service and more than 100 county agencies nationwide, as well as by at least 16 state correctional agencies including those in Alaska, California, Colorado, Delaware, Florida, Georgia, Kansas, Ohio, Washington and Wisconsin. It is also used on prisoners during judicial hearings, in breach of international standards on the treatment of prisoners.[45]

Supermaximum security units

Since the late 1980s the federal system and an increasing number of states have built so-called supermaximum security (or "supermax") facilities. These are designed for the long-term isolation of large numbers of prisoners whom the authorities consider to be too dangerous or disruptive to be held in the general population of maximum security prisons. In 1997, 36 states and the federal government were reported to

---

[44] Letter from M. Horn, Secretary of Corrections, 22 April 1998.

[45] The Standard Minimum Rules state that restraints "shall be removed when the prisoner appears before a judicial or administrative authority" (Rule 33 (a)).

operate at least 57 supermax facilities, housing more than 13,000 prisoners. Many more are under construction.[46]

Amnesty International recognizes that it is sometimes necessary to segregate prisoners for the safety of others or for their own protection. However, many aspects of the conditions in US supermax facilities violate international standards, and in some facilities conditions constitute cruel, inhuman or degrading treatment. Prolonged isolation in conditions of reduced sensory stimulation can cause severe physical and psychological damage.[47]

The UN Human Rights Committee stated in 1995 that conditions in certain US maximum security prisons were "incompatible" with international standards.[48] The UN Special Rapporteur on torture (an expert appointed by the UN Commission on Human Rights) reported in 1996 on cruel, inhuman and degrading treatment in H-Unit, Oklahoma, and Pelican Bay Security Housing Unit (SHU).[49]

Prisoners typically spend between 22 and 24 hours a day confined to small, solitary cells in which they eat, sleep and defecate. In many units, cells are considerably smaller than the 80 square feet (7.4 sq m) recommended as the minimum by the ACA, adding to the claustrophobic and unhealthy conditions.[50] In some units, cells have no windows to the outside and prisoners have little or no access to natural light or fresh air, in violation of international standards.[51] For example, prisoners in the Correctional Adjustment Center in Baltimore, Maryland, are confined in 65 sq ft (6 sq m), sealed, single cells. For several years they had no outside exercise until the Justice Department threatened a lawsuit. Prisoners are now allowed out of

---

[46] National Institute of Corrections, *Supermax Housing: A Survey of Current Practice*, March 1997, and Human Rights Watch, *Cold Storage: Super-Maximum Security Confinement in Indiana*, October 1997.

[47] For example, UK prisoners held in conditions similar to those in US supermax facilities have suffered disorders including impaired eyesight, weight loss, muscle wastage, memory loss and anaemia. See Amnesty International, *UK Special Security Units — Cruel, Inhuman and Degrading Treatment*, 1997 (AI Index: EUR 45/06/97).

[48] HRC Comments of 6 April 1995, UN Doc. CCPR/C/79/Add.50.

[49] UN Doc. E/CN.4/1996/35.

[50] Standard 3-4136, ACA Standards for Adult Correctional Institutions, 1990.

[51] Rule 11 of the Standard Minimum Rules states: "In all places where prisoners are required to live or work... windows shall be large enough to enable the prisoners to read or work by natural light, and shall be so constructed that they can allow the entrance of fresh air..."

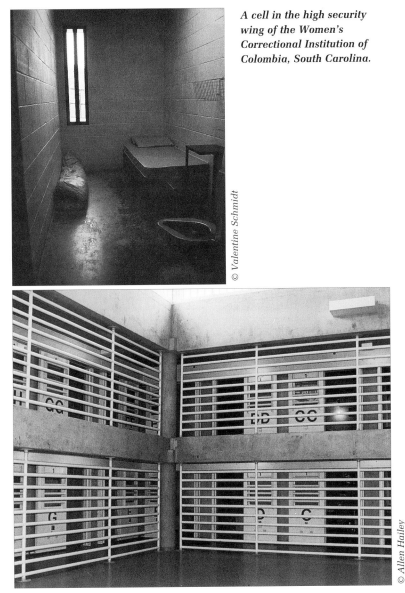

A cell in the high security wing of the Women's Correctional Institution of Colombia, South Carolina.

© Valentine Schmidt

© Allen Hailey

Several hundred death-row prisoners have been held in H-Unit at the Oklahoma State Penitentiary at McAlester since it opened more than seven years ago. They are held in windowless, concrete cells for 23 hours or more a day. Conditions in the unit have been condemned as cruel, inhuman and degrading by Amnesty International.

their cells for four to five hours a week, one hour of which must be outdoors.

In August 1997 Texas opened the W.J. Estelle High Security Unit, a 660-bed facility where prisoners are isolated in windowless cells for 23 hours or more a day. The concrete cells have no natural light and the solid steel doors have narrow slits which allow only a minimal view of the corridor outside.

Generally, supermax facilities provide no work, training or vocational programs. Opportunities for educational study are non-existent or extremely limited. The facilities are usually designed to minimize contact with other inmates and guards, with remote-controlled doors and video cameras replacing contact with staff. The cells tend to have solid steel doors rather than bars, cutting off sound and visual contact with others, including prisoners in the next cell. No televisions, radios, newspapers or books are allowed in the most restricted units. Contact with the outside world is also often severely limited and visits are usually conducted through a glass panel. In the Maximum Control Complex (MCC) at Westville, Indiana, prisoners were not allowed to wear watches or ask the time until a hunger-strike and a lawsuit led to some court-imposed changes. Many of these conditions are a flagrant breach of minimum international standards for the treatment of prisoners.[52]

US courts have ordered limited changes to the operation of some facilities. However, they have not ruled that confinement to supermax units is unconstitutional per se. In general, the courts have allowed states wide latitude in imposing restrictive conditions, including long-term isolation, when it is claimed that these serve legitimate security needs.

The length of time prisoners spend in supermax facilities varies. Many units do not provide any form of staged system that permits prisoners who behave well to move to less restrictive units. In some facilities, the process of review is discretionary, or the criteria for moving out of the units are vague or difficult to meet. Some prisoners may spend years in supermax units. In 22 jurisdictions, it is possible for inmates to complete their sentences in supermax housing and be released to the community without any transitional stage.[53]

The prison authorities state that inmates are placed in supermax

---

[52] Rules 77 (1) and 78 of the Standard Minimum Rules emphasize the importance of providing educational programs and recreational and cultural activities respectively. Rules 37 and 39 provide that prisoners should maintain contact with the outside world and be kept informed of news events.

[53] National Institute of Corrections, March 1997, op. cit.

units for reasons such as violent or predatory behaviour, repeated rule violations or attempted escapes. However, evidence suggests that many prisoners in supermax units have not warranted such a restrictive regime. For example, a number of states have moved all death row prisoners into supermax units, regardless of their disciplinary records. Prisoners may be assigned for long periods to the supermax unit in Wabash, Indiana, for relatively minor disciplinary infractions, such as insolence towards staff, and the period may be extended for transgressions committed there.[54] Others have reportedly been moved to supermax units because of overcrowding or because they have complained about prison conditions. Women in Valley State Prison, California, for example, have alleged that they were assigned, or threatened with assignment, to the supermax unit if they complained about sexual abuse by guards.[55] Some prisoners have reportedly been put in supermax units because of their political affiliations, although the broad grounds for confinement make such allegations difficult to verify.

Even mentally ill prisoners continue to be assigned to some supermax facilities despite evidence that the conditions are particularly damaging and inappropriate for them. Prison specialists say that mentally ill prisoners are more likely than other inmates to end up in such units because of behavioural difficulties in prison, and lack of resources to treat them. Other prisoners develop mental illness while in the unit.

Both the treatment for, and monitoring of, mental health are reported to be inadequate in many supermax facilities. The Justice Department found that psychotic inmates continued to be held at the Maryland supermax prison in 1996, despite the state's policy to exclude the mentally ill from the unit. Seriously mentally ill prisoners have been held in H-Unit, Oklahoma, without receiving appropriate evaluation or treatment.[56] Prisoners in MCC Westville were reportedly denied adequate mental health monitoring (as required under a court agreement) and many exhibited signs of mental illness.[57] Such

[54] Human Rights Watch, October 1997, op. cit.

[55] See, for example, S. Sadler, "Report from Valley State Prison for Women SHU", *Prison Focus*, Winter 1997. Amnesty International will publish a report on women in US prisons and jails in 1999.

[56] See Amnesty International, *USA: Conditions for death row prisoners in H-Unit, Oklahoma State Penitentiary,* 1994 (AI Index: AMR 51/34/94).

[57] Human Rights Watch, October 1997, op. cit.

lack of adequate evaluation of the mental health of prisoners in isolation is contrary to both international and US professional standards.[58]

Inadequate health care

Annette Romo, a young pregnant woman in a Maricopa jail, pleaded in vain with staff for medical help when she began bleeding in 1997. She eventually fell unconscious and was rushed to hospital. Her baby died.[59]

International standards clearly specify that medical care and treatment shall be provided whenever necessary, free of charge.[60] The Supreme Court has also ruled that inmates have a right to adequate medical care for "serious" medical needs. Despite this, in many cases prisons and jails have failed to meet the required standard. Correctional facilities are struggling to cope with the overall rise in the prison population and a growing number of inmates who require specialized care: people with substance abuse problems and related illnesses such as HIV/AIDs and tuberculosis; female inmates with health needs specific to women[61]; elderly prisoners; and inmates with mental health problems.[62]

Investigations, lawsuits and researchers have documented deficiencies in numerous facilities. These include: lack of screening for tuberculosis and other communicable diseases in overcrowded and insanitary jails; too few medical and psychiatric staff; failure to refer seriously ill inmates for treatment; delays in treatment or failure to deliver life-saving drugs; inadequate conditions for prisoners with HIV/AIDS; lack of access to gynaecological and obstetric services; and grossly deficient treatment for the mentally ill. Moreover, many states and local jails have started charging inmates fees for medical consultations, in violation of the international standards that medical care for prisoners should be free.[63]

---

[58] The NCCHC states that all inmates in disciplinary segregation should be evaluated by health personnel "prior to placement in segregation and daily while in segregation". (NCCHC Standards for Health Services in Prisons, 1997, p. 53). Rules 32 (3) of the Standard Minimum Rules requires prisoners in close confinement to be visited daily by the medical officer to assess their physical and mental health.

[59] At the time of writing, Arizona correctional authorities had not replied to Amnesty International's letters about Annette Romo's treatment.

[60] Principle 24 of the Body of Principles.

[61] Health issues will be examined in Amnesty International's March 1999 report on women in US prisons and jails.

[62] "Jails and prisons — America's new mental hospitals", *American Journal of Public Health*, Vol 85, No. 12, December 1995.

[63] Principle 24 of the Body of Principles.

The consequences of such failings can be fatal. Jane B., a 36-year-old mother of two serving a two-year sentence in a California prison, suffered from a severe gastro-intestinal disorder. Despite her requests for help, she was not given effective medical or psychological care. She slowly starved to death.[64]

Violations of children's rights

The ICCPR and other international standards require that incarcerated children[65] should be kept separate from adults (except where it is in the best interests of the child not to do so).[66] When the USA ratified the ICCPR, it reserved the right to treat juveniles as adults "in exceptional circumstances". Recent state legislation has increased the number of children held in adult facilities and proposed legislation would further weaken existing protection for children.[67]

Children prosecuted as adults

Under state and federal criminal laws, children above a specified age who are accused of specific serious offences (such as murder) may be prosecuted in the general criminal courts as adults.[68] In response to concerns about an increase in violent juvenile crime, the great majority of states have legislated in recent years to broaden the circumstances in which children may be prosecuted in the adult criminal justice system.

In at least 20 states, children who are convicted as adults may be sentenced to imprisonment in adult prisons and housed with adult

---

[64] The coroner's report indicated starvation as the cause of death. Jane B. was cited in a lawsuit (*Shumate v. Wilson*) to improve medical care in Californian women's prisons, which was settled in 1997 with the Corrections Department agreeing to a range of improvements. See E. Barry, "Women Prisoners and Health Care", in K. Moss ed., *Man-made Medicine*, Duke University Press, 1996.

[65] A child is defined in the Convention on the Rights of the Child as a person under the age of 18 unless, under the law applicable, majority is attained earlier.

[66] For example, ICCPR Articles 10 (2) (b) and 10 (3); Convention on the Rights of the Child Article 37(c).

[67] Amnesty International has a variety of concerns relating to the treatment of children by the US justice system. This report focuses on the incarceration of children in adult prisons and jails and the execution of juvenile offenders: a separate report is to be published in November 1998 covering a wider range of issues.

[68] The age varies between jurisdictions; some states do not specify a minimum age for certain crimes.

inmates.[69] In June 1998, more than 3,500 such children were in custody. Their welfare was of grave concern because of their extreme vulnerability to physical and sexual abuse by adults.[70]

At the time of writing, Congress was considering legislation designed to encourage the prosecution of children as adults under federal and state laws.[71]

Children in the juvenile justice system

For less serious offences, children are generally dealt with by special juvenile justice courts and institutions.

Until the mid-1970s, many of these children were held in adult jails for extended periods and had little or no separation from adult inmates. In response to evidence that children were being physically and sexually abused by adult inmates, and a high rate of suicides among children in jails, Congress legislated to provide a financial incentive to states to remove children from adult jails, and to keep children held in adult facilities completely separate. The legislation had a dramatic impact. All but two states (Wyoming and Kentucky) participate in the program and the degree of compliance with the requirements is high. However, the legislation being considered by Congress at the time of writing would significantly weaken the requirement that children and adults must be kept completely apart; the measure was opposed by a wide range of child welfare, legal and other organizations.

Mechanisms to remedy abuses

The appalling history of ill-treatment of prisoners around the world demonstrates that independent scrutiny is vital to prevent and stop

---

[69] Information provided by states in response to a telephone survey. Some states housed offenders under the age of 18 with other young offenders, generally aged up to 21 to 24. The 20 states are: Alabama, Florida, Idaho, Indiana, Iowa (soon to open a juvenile facility), Kansas, Minnesota (female only), Mississippi, Nebraska (soon to open a juvenile facility), Nevada, New Jersey, North Dakota, Oklahoma, Oregon, Pennsylvania, Rhode Island, South Dakota, Utah, Vermont and Wyoming.

[70] Abuse of juvenile prisoners by adults has been reported both in the USA and worldwide. See, for example, Report by (UN) Special Rapporteur on torture, UN Doc. E/CN.4/1988/17; Office of Juvenile Justice and Delinquency Prevention, "Meeting the Mandates", *Juvenile Justice*, Volume II, Number 2, Fall/Winter 1995.

[71] Violent and Juvenile Offender Act of 1997; see Report of the Committee on the Judiciary, United States Senate, Report 105-108, 9 October 1997.

serious abuses in correctional facilities. International standards therefore provide that "places of detention shall be visited regularly by qualified and experienced persons appointed by, and responsible to, a competent authority distinct from the authority directly in charge of the administration of the place of detention or imprisonment."[72] Unfortunately, the reality in the USA falls far short of this standard, particularly in relation to jails.

Most prisons and jails in the country have internal mechanisms for investigating complaints. Self-monitoring, however, is not enough. Internal inquiries have often been ineffectual and guards have systematically attempted to cover up abuses. Fear of retaliation has often prevented inmates from filing grievances within the system.

State monitoring bodies

There are a large number and wide variety of monitoring bodies in the USA. They include inspection agencies within departments of correction, and legally established bodies outside departments of correction, such as ombudsman offices. In some states, such as Illinois, certain nongovernmental organizations have the right to inspect facilities.

However, there are significant gaps in the coverage, resources and effectiveness of these agencies. Among the most notable are:

- 14 states do not have any jail inspection program;[73]
- in some states jail inspections are limited to building audits, such as checking compliance with fire regulations;
- jail and prison inspection bodies generally lack the power to force facilities to make necessary changes;
- inspection bodies have inadequate resources to monitor effectively the growing number of jails, prisons and inmates, and some
- inspection bodies have had their resources cut;
- the objectivity of some inspection agencies is suspect because they generally employ investigators who are former correctional or law enforcement officers and so are likely to give more credence to correctional officers than to inmates.

---

[72] Principle 29, Body of Principles.

[73] Arizona, Colorado, Georgia, Kansas, Mississippi, Missouri, Montana, Nevada, New Hampshire, New Mexico, South Dakota, Washington, West Virginia, Wyoming. See American Correctional Association, *1996-1998 National Jail and Adult Detention Directory*, Maryland, 1996.

UNITED STATES OF AMERICA

National standards associations

Nationally, a limited monitoring role is undertaken by the ACA and the NCCHC, which periodically inspect jails and prisons that are accredited with them. Amnesty International and others have expressed concern both about some of the standards and about the monitoring process. During its investigation into conditions in H-Unit, Oklahoma, Amnesty International found certain ACA standards to be deficient.[74] Some experts believe that standards have been weakened in response to the pressure the authorities face in coping with the rapid rise in the number of inmates: "Unfortunately, the desire for accreditation recognition became so strong and compliance often so difficult that administrative pressure from the field was brought to bear to lower standards so that compliance could be more easily achieved."[75]

The courts

In the absence of effective state and national monitoring bodies, prisoners have turned to the courts. The most important have been the federal courts, which include the Supreme Court, where inmates have sued for violations of rights enshrined in the Constitution. Since the late 1960s litigation has been widely used to obtain improvements in conditions. Almost every state has been, or still is, involved in litigation dealing with conditions in its prisons, and many jails have been placed under court orders requiring improvements.[76]

While litigation can be a very effective way to remedy abuses, it is slow and difficult to use. Major cases are extremely expensive and may take years to reach a conclusion. Settlements are individually framed and do not have binding effect on other facilities. Unless the Supreme Court has made a ruling on a particular issue, even similar complaints may be handled differently in different jurisdictions.

Legal action by prisoners seeking redress has been significantly restricted in recent years by both judicial and legislative decisions. Led by the Supreme Court in a number of cases, the federal courts have increasingly taken a view which observers have characterized as meaning that they "must defer to the judgment of correctional administrators

---

[74] See Amnesty International, 1994, op.cit.

[75] See Breed, "Corrections: A Victim of Situational Ethics", *Crime and Delinquency*, Vol 44, No.1, January 1998.

[76] American Correctional Association, *1997 Directory —Juvenile and adult correctional departments, institutions, agencies and paroling authorities*, Maryland, 1997.

in all but the most extreme cases".[77] This self-imposed limitation on the role of the courts has been complemented by two laws passed by Congress in 1996.

One measure prohibits the Legal Services Corporation, a federal agency that provides legal services to poor people, from providing funds to legal aid organizations that represent prisoners in cases relating to their conditions. The second measure, the Prison Litigation Reform Act, limits the power of the federal courts to improve prison conditions by: preventing the courts from enforcing voluntary agreements; requiring the dismissal of court orders after two years (rarely enough time to fix serious problems); preventing prisoners from bringing cases alleging mental or emotional harm unless they can also prove physical injury (prohibiting lawsuits involving psychological torture); making it more difficult and more expensive for individual prisoners to bring cases to court; and limiting the fees for attorneys who represent prisoners in successful civil rights cases (making it more difficult to secure experienced lawyers).

These restrictions on court powers and access to courts increase the risk of human rights abuse. According to observers, "without the threat of being held accountable before a federal court, the quality of jail and prison operations may begin to deteriorate...The 'get tough on inmates' mood, combined with decreasing levels of accountability for maintaining some level of minimum standards, raises the spectre of decreased funding for jails, corresponding cutbacks in staff and training, and the rebirth of the sorts of very brutal, barbaric, and often dangerous conditions that led to the initial wave of court intervention in the early 1970s."[78]

Justice Department

Under the Civil Rights of Institutionalized Persons Act of 1980 (CRIPA), the Justice Department is entitled to investigate conditions of confinement in prisons and jails and other institutions, if it receives information that prisoners are being systematically deprived of their constitutional or federal rights. If it finds that the conditions violate laws, it may negotiate with the authorities to correct the violation or, if negotiation fails, seek court orders. The Justice Department may also bring criminal civil rights charges against state officials who violate the constitutional

---

[77] W. Collins and A. Collins, *Women in jail: legal issues*, National Institute of Corrections, Washington DC, 1996.

[78] Ibid.

rights of others while acting under "color of law". At the end of 1997, Justice Department officials informed Amnesty International that more than 300 facilities had been investigated since the enactment of CRIPA.

Most Justice Department investigations that find violations are resolved through consent decrees (voluntary agreements). However, the Justice Department has recently noted "increased unwillingness by states to correct deficiencies voluntarily, necessitating litigation".[79] Since 1996, Justice Department investigators have been denied access to facilities by at least two states — Arizona and Michigan — and were initially refused access to the Maryland Correctional Adjustment (supermax) facility.

Requests to the Justice Department to initiate new investigations far outweigh its capacity to respond. The process from initial investigation to the negotiation and monitoring of agreements is generally lengthy, and in recent years the other responsibilities of the section of the Justice Department that deals with CRIPA cases have significantly expanded.

The independence and powers of the Justice Department make it a critical component of the mechanisms for the redress of abuses in correctional facilities. It is imperative that the Executive and Congress ensure that it receives adequate funding to undertake this important task effectively.

Recommendations

Federal, state and local authorities should develop, implement and rigorously enforce standards for correctional facilities that are consistent with international human rights standards for the treatment of prisoners, and which forbid torture and cruel, inhuman or degrading treatment.

1. The authorities should make clear that brutality and excessive force will not be tolerated and should establish independent bodies to investigate all allegations of abuse thoroughly and impartially. Officials responsible for abuses — including failure to report misconduct — should be disciplined and, where appropriate, prosecuted.

2. The authorities should take all measures to make sure that rape and other sexual abuse of inmates by staff or other inmates does not take place in correctional facilities. All alleged incidents should be independently investigated and those responsible brought to justice.

---

[79] Justice Department Budget Request and Report to Congress, 1997.

3. Federal, state and local authorities should ensure that adequate medical care is provided whenever necessary, free of charge. Health care and treatment should accord with professionally recognized standards. Medical personnel who have grounds for suspecting that torture or ill-treatment have taken place should be required to report cases to independent authorities.

4. Measures to prevent and punish torture and ill-treatment, including rape and other sexual abuse, of women should include an explicit prohibition of all forms of sexual abuse by staff; informing staff and inmates of inmates rights' and that offenders will be subject to punishment; restricting the role of male staff with regard to female inmates in line with Rule 53 of the Standard Minimum Rules for the Treatment of Prisoners; investigating all complaints in line with best practice for the investigation of sexual assault; protecting women who make complaints from retaliation; and providing appropriate redress and care to victims of abuse. The routine use of restraints on pregnant women should be prohibited, and women should never be restrained during labour; restraints should only be used on pregnant women as a last resort and should never put the safety of a woman or the foetus at risk. Health care for female inmates should meet recognized community standards and should recognize the particular health needs of women.

5. Children in prisons and jails should be completely separated from adults, unless it is considered in the child's best interests not to do so.

6. The authorities in charge of supermax units should amend their policies to ensure that no prisoner is confined long-term or indefinitely in conditions of isolation and reduced sensory stimulation. The authorities should improve conditions in such units so that prisoners have more out-of-cell time; better access to fresh air and natural light; improved exercise facilities; increased association, where possible, with other inmates and access to work, training or vocational programs; and are not held in windowless cells. The mentally ill or those at risk of mental illness should be removed from supermax units. The authorities should establish clear criteria for and regular review of placement in supermax units.

7. The authorities should ban the use of remote control electroshock stun belts by law enforcement and correctional agencies.

Law enforcement and correctional agencies should suspend the use of other electro-shock weapons pending the outcome of a rigorous, independent and impartial inquiry into the use and effects of the equipment.

8. The federal authorities should establish an independent review of the use of OC (pepper) spray by law enforcement and correctional agencies. Authorities who continue to authorize the spray should introduce strict guidelines and limitations on its use, with clear monitoring procedures.

9. Four-point restraints should only be used when strictly necessary as an emergency short-term measure to prevent damage or injury, and in accordance with international and US professional medical standards. The federal authorities should institute an urgent national inquiry into the use of restraint chairs in prisons and jails.

10. Federal and state authorities should establish and fund agencies completely independent of correctional authorities to monitor conditions in prisons and jails, with powers to take action to remedy problems.

11. The federal government and Congress should use their legislative, financial and other powers to encourage, and if necessary require, recalcitrant states to comply fully with international standards for the protection of the rights of people in prisons and jails.

12. The federal government should review the impact of legislation which restricts inmates, access to courts, including the Prison Litigation Reform Act, and ask Congress to amend provisions that have unduly restricted inmates' ability to use the courts to end ill-treatment. The federal government and Congress should provide the necessary additional funds to allow the Justice Department to fulfill its mandate under the Civil Rights of Institutionalized Persons Act of 1980 to investigate conditions in correctional facilities and to take action when necessary.

5

TREATED AS CRIMINALS: Asylum-seekers in the USA

"Everyone says America is the place for human rights. I thought maybe I had arrived in the wrong country."

A refugee who was detained in harsh conditions for 14 months before being granted asylum.

Everyone has the right to seek and to enjoy asylum if they are forced to flee their country to escape persecution. The USA accepts this principle, and has agreed to be bound by international standards to protect refugees.[1] Yet US authorities frequently violate the fundamental human rights of asylum-seekers by detaining them simply for seeking asylum.

Asylum-seekers are not criminals. But an increasing number of asylum-seekers are placed behind bars when they arrive in the USA. They are often detained indefinitely, and many are held on grounds beyond those allowed by international standards. Many are confined with criminal prisoners, but unlike criminal suspects, are often denied bail and have no idea when they will be released. They are held in conditions that are sometimes inhuman and degrading. Asylum-seekers in the USA are liable to be treated like criminals: stripped and searched; shackled and chained; sometimes verbally or physically abused. They are often denied access to their families, lawyers and non-governmental organizations (NGOs) who could help them.

The US government is obliged to ensure that no one is returned to a country where they would be at risk of persecution and that all asylum-seekers have access to a fair and satisfactory asylum determination procedure. Amnesty International calls on the US authorities to ensure that asylum-seekers are detained **only** when a legitimate reason for doing so has been demonstrated (and only when other measures short of detention will not suffice, and only for a minimal

---

[1] In 1968 the USA acceded to the 1967 Protocol to the 1951 UN Convention relating to the Status of Refugees (1951 Refugee Convention), by which it undertook to apply Articles 2 to 34 of the 1951 Refugee Convention.

period). In particular, the practice of holding asylum-seekers in jails should be stopped. Children should neither be separated from their families nor detained. All detained asylum-seekers should have adequate access to the outside world.

Behind bars: detention of asylum-seekers

US policies and practices, which result in the indefinite detention of most of those who seek asylum in the USA, violate international human rights standards.[2]

The international body with statutory responsibility for refugees is the Office of the UN High Commissioner for Refugees (UNHCR). The USA is a member of UNHCR's Executive Committee (EXCOM), an intergovernmental body of more than 50 states. EXCOM's conclusions, which are adopted by consensus, are regarded as authoritative in the field of refugee rights.[3]

EXCOM has stressed that national legislation and administrative practices should differentiate refugees and asylum-seekers from other aliens, because of the fundamental distinction between refugees in need of international protection and other migrants.[4]

EXCOM has stated that the detention of asylum-seekers "should normally be avoided".[5] Detention is allowed by international standards only:

- if it is necessary, and
- if it is lawful and not arbitrary, and
- if it is for one of the following reasons:
  (i) "to verify identity";

---

[2] International standards define refugees' rights and limit states' use of detention. Article 9 of the Universal Declaration of Human Rights provides that "No one shall be subjected to arbitrary arrest, detention or exile". More detailed safeguards are included in other instruments, such as the 1951 Refugee Convention and its 1967 Protocol, and the ICCPR. Article 31 of the 1951 Refugee Convention exempts refugees coming directly from a country of persecution from being punished on account of their illegal entry or presence, provided that they present themselves without delay to the authorities and show good cause.

[3] In addition, Article 35 of the 1951 Refugee Convention obliges states parties to "cooperate with [UNHCR] in... supervising the application of the provisions of [the] Convention."

[4] US legislation uses the term "alien" to denote various types of non-citizens, including asylum-seekers. Amnesty International describes those who claim asylum as asylum-seekers, and those who have been granted recognition as refugees.

[5] EXCOM Conclusion 44.

(ii) "to determine the elements on which the claim to refugee status or asylum is based";

(iii) "to deal with cases where refugees or asylum-seekers have destroyed their travel or identity documents or have used fraudulent documents in order to mislead the authorities of the State in which they intend to claim asylum";

(iv) "to protect national security or public order".[6]

The onus is on detaining authorities to demonstrate why measures short of detention are not sufficient. Even if asylum-seekers are detained legitimately, detention should not continue for longer than is necessary.

Many of these elements are breached by US detention practices: the authorities detain asylum-seekers on grounds beyond those outlined above, and decisions to detain or to continue detention are often arbitrary.

A new immigration act has led to a further sharp rise in detentions. In 1996 Congress enacted the Illegal Immigration Reform and Immigrant Responsibility Act (IIRIRA)[7] which contains "expedited removal provisions". These allow the summary return of people seeking to enter the USA without valid documents. Under these expedited removal provisions, even asylum-seekers who manage to convince officials that they have a "credible fear" of returning to their country are generally detained until their case has been finally decided, which may take months or even years. The IIRIRA punishes breaches of immigration procedures. Yet for many refugees the only way to escape the risk of imprisonment, torture or death in their country of origin is to use false documents or to obtain a visa on false pretences.

The number of those detained under the authority of the Immigration and Naturalization Services (INS) has soared, rising by 75 per cent between 1996 and 1998. In early 1998 the INS had "bed spaces" for an estimated 15,050 detainees and the INS anticipated that this would rise to 24,000 by the year 2001, when it is expected that most of the detainees will be held in jails.[8] The lack of coherent official data makes it impossible to ascertain how many are asylum-seekers.

---

[6] EXCOM Conclusion 44b.

[7] In 1980 Congress amended the Immigration and Nationality Act, which governs immigration and refugee issues, to bring it into line with the 1967 Protocol. However, the IIRIRA significantly revised the Immigration and Nationality Act, lessening protection for refugees.

[8] Justice Department, "Federal Detention Plan", May 1997. INS detainees include asylum-seekers and other immigration detainees. See "Interpreter Releases", Vol. 75, No. 18, May 11, 1998.

Lack of oversight

There are four main types of detention facilities where asylum-seekers are incarcerated in the USA: state and local county jails; INS "service processing centres" (SPCs); private contract facilities; and Federal Bureau of Prisons (BOP) prisons. There are also a variety of juvenile detention facilities used to hold children and unaccompanied minors.

The INS relies heavily on standards produced by the American Correctional Association (ACA) for holding prisoners, standards inappropriate for the situation of refugees. In practice, standards, accountability and conditions of detention vary greatly in different types of facility, and there is no national system to oversee and hold accountable those responsible for the detention and treatment of asylum-seekers.[9]

The INS has recently proposed new detention standards, which, if followed, will be an improvement on existing practices.[10] However, these standards do not apply to jails, where about half of all INS detainees are currently held. Moreover, the monitoring of these new standards is delegated to INS Officers in Charge — the very people in charge of INS detention facilities.

Monitoring of facilities where asylum-seekers are held is inadequate: "INS officials concede that it reviews local jails at most once a year based on a check-list that does not require 100 per cent compliance. Appointed by the [INS] District Director, monitoring teams announce their visits in advance and view themselves as 'guests'."[11]

Lack of support

"It was easier to have access to my client on death row than to an asylum-seeker in the New Orleans jail."

> The lawyer of a Somali refugee held in
> four different states while seeking asylum.

The US authorities have failed to ensure that all asylum-seekers have access to outside assistance — assistance to which they are entitled.

---

[9] The INS uses the American Correctional Association (ACA) Standards for Adult Local Detention Centres as the model for its own SPCs and for private contract facilities. BOP facilities use their own standards. The INS reviews state and local jails based on ACA standards.

[10] Standards issued to date include: telephone access, group rights presentations, media access, recreation, access to legal materials, medical care, clothing and bedding, religious practices, suicide prevention, hunger strikes, voluntary work and marriage requests.

[11] See, D. Kerwin, "Interpreter Releases", Vol. 75, No. 18, May 11, 1998 at 658, fn 99.

© Barbara Karl/SND

Detainees at the Port Isabel, Texas INS (Immigration and Naturalization Service) facility. The authorities do not identify and separate asylum-seekers from other detainees, and lawyers and advocates are often denied access to them.

Asylum-seekers are frequently denied access to visitors, to lawyers, to interpreters, to representatives from NGOs and other care-givers. Some face obstacles in making telephone calls and receiving letters or information essential for them to support their asylum claim.

Basic information, such as lists of lawyers and NGOs willing to assist asylum-seekers, may not be provided at all. How can asylum-seekers find legal or other assistance when held in remote detention facilities, with little or no English, no money, limited access to a telephone and no useful information about who can help them with their asylum case?

Some detention facilities refuse to allow lawyers access to asylum-seekers, others allow it only reluctantly, making lawyers and detainees wait for hours to meet. Anastasia, a refugee from Liberia detained in a county jail in Texas, said that after a visit from her lawyer, she was left in the tiny interview room for four hours and taunted by prison guards. She said she discouraged further visits, because she was afraid of repercussions. Anastasia was released after three months but her husband remained in an INS service processing centre. Visitors had to line up for hours in the hot sun for a visit lasting 20 or 30 minutes. Anastasia was not allowed to touch her husband, not even hold his hand, and was not allowed to give him basic hygiene products such as skin cream and a hairbrush.

Asylum-seekers are shunted from one facility to another, across state lines, without any explanation other than that their bed space was needed. Little or no effort is made to keep asylum-seekers close to their families or sources of legal representation or to notify them that the asylum-seeker has been moved. Some asylum-seekers told Amnesty International that they thought they had been moved from one facility to another as punishment.

Many asylum-seekers have been traumatized by the events that forced them to uproot themselves and flee. Being held behind bars in the country where they sought freedom is bad enough; being cut off from all external forms of support exacerbates their continuing trauma.

Indefinite detention

Asylum-seekers in detention, unlike other prisoners, have no idea when they will be released. They have committed no criminal offence in exercising their right to flee their homes and seek protection elsewhere, but are indefinitely deprived of their liberty. They are subject to apparently arbitrary judgments by INS officials who, in some cases, seem to operate as a law unto themselves.

To ensure that detention lasts only as long as necessary, the reasons for detention and its necessity should be automatically reviewed at regular intervals by a judicial or similar authority. This does not happen under current law or practice. Decisions on continuation of detention rest with INS officials, not judicial officials, and practices vary considerably from district to district and even within districts. For example, several Cubans were released from detention in Miami, while others, who had arrived on the same boat in late 1996, but had been transferred to detention facilities elsewhere in Florida (within the same INS district), were effectively denied the possibility of release.

There is no system in place to review detention decisions in many, if not most, INS jurisdictions. Release options and how to request them are often not revealed to asylum-seekers. Deportation Officers are often the only source of information, and they may be inaccessible. A detainee claiming to speak for 400 people held in an INS facility in California gave the refusal of Deportation Officers to communicate as one reason for their hunger strike in June 1998.

According to international law there must be an opportunity for a review of the decision to detain which examines the merits of the case, not just procedural correctness. The US practice fails to examine the overall circumstances of the asylum-seeker and the necessity of continuing detention. Under US procedures, asylum-seekers' detention may be subject to review at the discretion of local authorities, but in the few cases where detention is reviewed and parole recommended, many are unable to satisfy the bail requirements or other criteria to gain release. For example, U.D., a diplomat from Uganda who entered the USA with a valid diplomatic passport and a valid visitor's visa, was still detained five months after arriving in New York and seeking asylum. He had established a credible fear of persecution, had confirmed his identity, had community ties in the USA and was not suspected of any offence. Yet he remained confined in the Wackenhut facility, Queens, New York, as of April 1998.

In Pennsylvania, the INS refused to parole an asylum-seeker with a heart condition, although his wife lived in Canada and his lawyer had arranged for him to be taken to the Canadian border. He collapsed and died of a heart attack in May 1996 after being in detention for more than a year.

Sometimes a decision is made to refuse release on the grounds that the asylum-seeker may abscond; sometimes the decision-maker is ignorant about the country from which the asylum-seeker fled, and about US law and policy. The asylum-seeker often does not have adequate legal representation when such critical decisions are made.

Information from the INS suggests that the majority of asylum-seekers who have established that they have a credible fear of persecution within their country of origin remain in detention, while they wait for a final determination of their asylum claim.

In some cases the INS holds people in detention even though they have been granted asylum by immigration judges, while it appeals against the decision. For example, Sai Qing Jiang, a Chinese woman who arrived in the USA in March 1997 without valid documents, was jailed in Bakersfield, California. In August 1997 she was granted asylum, but the INS would not release her pending their appeal against the decision. The letter denying her release said: "By denying parole, I will discourage aliens from attempting to enter the United States through unlawful means as this applicant has done."[12]

[12]Letter from San Francisco INS District Director, Thomas J. Schiltgen, 5 September 1997.

Treated as criminals

Officials in charge of the detention of asylum-seekers do not differentiate between asylum-seekers and other detainees. As a result asylum-seekers are subject to the same treatment as other prisoners, especially when held in jails — treatment which may include shackling, solitary confinement and body searches.

Asylum-seekers should never be held in prisons or jails. A prison is not a suitable place in which to detain someone who is neither convicted nor suspected of a criminal offence. In the limited circumstances when it is permissible to detain asylum-seekers, they should be accommodated in facilities specifically designed for that purpose and staffed by suitably qualified personnel mindful of their special circumstances. Asylum-seekers face particular difficulties in detention because of language barriers, their personal experience of human rights abuse, and the fact that they are detained indefinitely.

Conditions of Detention

There is no consistency across the USA in how detained asylum-seekers are treated. While conditions are not harsh in all facilities, Amnesty International has documented instances of overcrowding, lack of access to daylight, exercise and recreational facilities, and, in some cases, verbal or physical abuse by staff.[13] Many detainees are held in dormitory style rooms which offer no privacy as bathrooms and showers are in open view and beds (or bunk beds) are in close proximity.[14]

"They took me to Esmor. Esmor was a terrible place... All day we were locked inside. It was cold in the winter, there was no heat. The snow and rain came inside the room. Day and night I cried, because it seems no one cares what is happening to me.

"The guards treated us like we were big criminals. They were always telling us to shut up. There was no door to the shower. Sometimes when the girls were taking showers, the men guards would walk into the office next to the room and look inside.

[13] In May 1997 Amnesty International visited a variety of detention facilities used to detain immigrants and asylum-seekers. Further information has been supplied by other NGOs with access to detention facilities.

[14] Officials recognize the problem of overcrowding: in June 1995 officials at the Krome SPC removed detainees to deceive a congressional delegation regarding problems in the facility. Bromwich, Inspector General, Alleged Deception of Congress: The Congressional Task Force on Immigration Reform's Fact Finding Visit to the Miami District of INS, June 1996.

"One day the guards were doing a search. They took us into a big room and began to check all our things, the sheets and blankets. We were there for a long time and I was sick that day. I asked for some water. Then the guard grabbed my hair and she kicked me in the stomach and in the legs and on the head. After she beat me, they took me to the isolation room for a day and half."

Hawa Abdi Jama, a Somali refugee held in New Jersey in 1994

An official investigation confirmed much of Hawa Abdi Jama's testimony. It revealed widespread abuse of detainees including "harassment, verbal abuse and other degrading actions" by guards and sub-standard medical care.[15]

Conditions in many detention centres have continued to deteriorate under the pressure of rising numbers. Asylum-seekers, some emotionally disturbed, some deeply traumatized, reported that they spent 24 hours a day for weeks on end crowded into one room, without access to fresh air or natural light. Many asylum-seekers are also subjected to frequent strip searches and are shackled and handcuffed if they are taken to hearings or appointments outside the jail or detention centre.

Women

Women asylum-seekers are more likely to be detained together with criminal offenders than men. Their access to legal and social assistance is limited or non-existent. Because there are usually small numbers of women asylum-seekers held in a given jail, the problem of isolation is particularly acute for these women. They often cannot communicate in English, and find the environment terrifying.[16]

One asylum-seeker told Amnesty International that she was frequently threatened by her fellow inmates, was made to sleep on the floor for two months and felt at risk of sexual assault. Others reported that they were denied basic sanitary products: one said she had been yelled at by the prison guard when she stained her prison clothes after her repeated requests for sanitary products had been ignored. Detainees said they were given only one change of prison clothing a month, were not given soap and were placed in solitary confinement for minor transgressions of prison rules that they did not understand.

---

[15] INS Assessment Team, *The Elizabeth New Jersey Contract Detention Facility Operated by ESMOR Inc.*, (Interim Report), July 1995, page 5. (The INS has since cancelled its contract with ESMOR Inc.)

[16] See *Liberty Denied: Women Seeking Asylum Imprisoned in the United States*, Women's Commission for Refugee Women and Children, April 1997.

Visiting room in the York County Prison in Pennsylvania. Detainees are separated from visitors by bullet-proof glass; many asylum-seekers are held in maximum security facilities and subjected to the same conditions as high-risk criminal prisoners.

Children

Children who need protection from persecution in their country of origin reportedly continue to be separated from their families and held in prison-like conditions, in breach of international standards.[17] The USA's

---

[17] The UN Convention on the Rights of the Child specifies that refugee children should receive "appropriate protection and humanitarian assistance" (Article 22); the UN Rules for the Protection of Juveniles Deprived of their Liberty provide that "deprivation of the liberty of a juvenile should be a disposition of last resort and for the minimum necessary period and should be limited to exceptional cases" (Article 2); and the ICCPR requires that: "juvenile offenders shall be segregated from adults and be accorded treatment appropriate to their age and legal status" (Article 10(3)).

obligations towards refugee children, as defined by the international community, are based on the principle that the best interests of the child should be paramount and on the understanding that imprisonment of any juvenile should be a last resort.

Children who have been through the trauma of being driven from their homes in fear and who find themselves alone in a strange land need special help. Too often they are not getting it in the USA. For example, 13-year-old Rajakumar fled from Sri Lanka with his mother after his father had been seized by government soldiers and "disappeared". He and his mother arrived in the USA in March 1998. Rajakumar was locked for more than one month in a New York hotel room with a group of strangers. He had limited telephone contact with his mother but was then moved without her knowledge to an INS juvenile facility in Florida. His mother was frantic with worry about him, and although she was granted asylum, the INS continued to detain her while they appealed against the decision. The two were finally released from detention and reunited only after sustained legal intervention.

The staff in juvenile correctional facilities are not generally equipped or trained to deal with refugee children. Confinement in a juvenile correctional facility, with juvenile offenders, is not appropriate treatment for such children.

The USA should ratify the Convention on the Rights of the Child, the main international human rights treaty protecting all children's rights. The authorities should ensure that minors are not separated from their families — in exceptional cases where detention may be necessary and justified, families should be placed in family centres. Children should be detained only as a last resort and in facilities appropriate to their vulnerability. In all cases, the authorities should strive to uphold the physical and mental well-being of the child.

Unaccompanied minors who arrive in the USA to seek asylum should have automatic legal representation, and guardianship arrangements to protect their interests should be put in place.

Recommendations

International standards guarantee everyone the right to seek and to enjoy asylum from persecution, and provide that no one should be returned to a country where they would be at risk of human rights violations. They require that the detention of asylum-seekers should normally be avoided. If detention is necessary, this should be demonstrated by means of a prompt, fair individual hearing before a judicial or similar authority whose status and tenure afford the strongest possible guarantees of competence, impartiality and independence. The decision to detain should be reviewed regularly by an independent body. Asylum-seekers should be advised of the reasons for their detention, of their rights and release options, and of access to assistance.

In line with these minimum international standards, Amnesty International believes that the US authorities should institute systems to differentiate between asylum-seekers and other migrants, and should treat them according to international standards for the protection of refugees, whether they are held in private or public facilities. In particular:

1. The practice of holding asylum-seekers in jails should be ended. If detention is necessary and justified, asylum-seekers should be detained in facilities appropriate to their circumstances, in line with international standards.

2. Asylum-seekers should be allowed adequate access to counsel and others who could provide assistance at all stages of the asylum procedure. NGOs should be given ready access to any facility where asylum-seekers are detained.

3. Children seeking asylum should be detained only as a last resort and in facilities appropriate to their status. They should not be separated from their families. Guardianship arrangements should be made to protect their interests.

4. Asylum-seekers who have demonstrated a "credible fear" of persecution should be released unless there are exceptional and compelling reasons to keep them in detention. An INS appeal against a decision to grant asylum may never be used to justify continued detention. The procedure for examining the validity of detention (the so-called "asylum pre-screening process") should be stipulated in binding regulations and should require any detention of asylum-seekers to be justified in line with international standards.

5. The INS, as the body responsible for protecting the rights of asylum-seekers, should be publicly accountable for its fulfilment of this obligation. Conditions of detention for asylum-seekers — regardless of the type of facility in which they are held — should be monitored by an independent and impartial body, using standards appropriate to the situation of asylum-seekers.

6

THE DEATH PENALTY: Arbitrary, unfair and racially biased

More than 350 people have been executed in the USA since 1990. The USA has the highest known death row population on earth: over 3,300 people await their deaths at the hands of US authorities.

International human rights standards seek to restrict the scope of the death penalty. They forbid its use against juvenile offenders, see it as an unacceptable punishment for the mentally impaired, and demand the highest legal safeguards for all capital trials. The USA fails to meet these minimum standards on all counts.

Any justice system can be vulnerable to the pressures of economics, politics or prejudice. In the USA a defendant who cannot afford a competent lawyer is more likely to be sentenced to death than someone with more money. Whether or not a defendant is sentenced to death may be more influenced by the fact that a prosecutor or judge is due for re-election and wants to appear "tough on crime", than by the gravity of the offence. The way the death penalty has been used in the USA has consistently been shown to be racist. As the authorities attempt to speed up the time between sentence and execution, the risk of killing the innocent is increasing.

Many of the people on death row have been responsible for brutal crimes with tragic ramifications for the families and loved ones of the victims. As an organization dedicated to the victims of human rights violations, Amnesty International would never seek to excuse or belittle these crimes. But human rights are the basic rights to which all human beings are entitled, no matter who they are or what they may have done.

Amnesty International believes that the US government and state authorities should take immediate steps to abolish the death penalty as it violates fundamental human rights.

International trends

"Every person shall have the right to life. If not, the killer unwittingly achieves a final and perverse moral

victory by making the state a killer too, thus reducing social abhorrence at the conscious extinction of human beings."

Justice Sachs, South African Constitutional Court, 1995

The South African Constitutional Court unanimously ruled in 1995 that the death penalty for murder violated the country's Constitution. In 1998 any such ruling in the USA seems a distant hope. For since South Africa abandoned capital punishment, the USA has joined the tiny group of nations responsible for the vast majority of the world's judicial killings. In 1997 the USA carried out 74 executions — the highest number for four decades. Only China, Saudi Arabia and Iran were known to have executed more prisoners.

More than 100 countries have now abolished the death penalty in law or practice. In April 1998 the UN Commission on Human Rights adopted a resolution calling on all member states which still use the death penalty to establish a moratorium on executions, with a view to

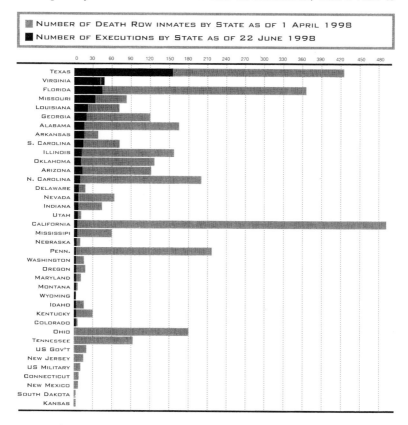

NUMBER OF DEATH ROW INMATES BY STATE AS OF 1 APRIL 1998
NUMBER OF EXECUTIONS BY STATE AS OF 22 JUNE 1998

abolishing the death penalty altogether. Against the global trend towards abolition, however, the USA has relentlessly increased its rate of executions and the number of crimes punishable by death.

The ramifications of the use of the death penalty in a country as influential as the USA go far beyond its borders. Officials in different countries have suggested that it is either a factor in, or justification for, their own decision to retain the punishment. In 1997 government officials from both the Philippines and Guatemala reportedly inspected execution chambers in the USA as part of their research into lethal injection as a method for killing condemned prisoners. At least one Philippines official was reported to have witnessed an execution in Texas during his trip. Both Guatemala and the Philippines have since adopted lethal injections.

In 1948 the USA played a leading role in the adoption of the Universal Declaration of Human Rights, which proclaims the right of every human being to life and freedom from cruel, inhuman or degrading treatment or punishment. Yet in 1998 most US political leaders do not even consider the death penalty to be a human rights issue. So while it is unconstitutional for the state of Florida to administer electricity to torture a prisoner, it remains acceptable, even a vote winner, for it to do so to cause death.

History repeats itself

"Twenty years have passed since this Court declared that the death penalty must be imposed fairly, and with reasonable consistency or not at all, and despite the effort of the states and the courts to devise legal formulas and procedural rules to meet this daunting challenge, the death penalty remains fraught with arbitrariness, discrimination, caprice and mistake... I feel morally and intellectually obligated simply to concede that the death penalty experiment has failed."

Justice Blackmun, US Supreme Court, 1994

In 1972 the US Supreme Court struck down the country's death penalty laws[1] on the grounds that they were being administered in an "arbitrary and capricious" manner, violating the US Constitution. Several states subsequently passed new laws, which in 1976 the Supreme Court ruled were constitutional as they allowed the death penalty to be applied with "guided discretion"[2]. By 1998, laws allowing for the use of the death penalty existed in 38 states, and under federal and military law.

---

[1] *Furman v. Georgia.*

[2] *Gregg v. Georgia.*

UNITED STATES OF AMERICA

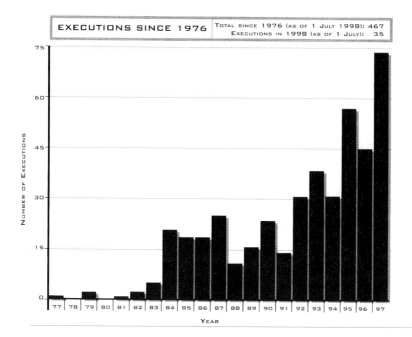

EXECUTIONS SINCE 1976
TOTAL SINCE 1976 (AS OF 1 JULY 1998): 467
EXECUTIONS IN 1998 (AS OF 1 JULY): 35

NUMBER OF EXECUTIONS

YEAR

Although the Supreme Court's 1976 ruling specified that guided discretion must be applied in the imposition of the death penalty, many states have undermined this ruling by greatly expanding their original death penalty statutes. For example, Illinois reintroduced the death penalty in 1977 with six categories of capital murder. By 1998 this had increased to 17. Likewise, Pennsylvania has expanded its capital murder categories from eight in 1978 to 17 in 1998.

In reality the death penalty is administered in the USA today in much the same way as it was in 1972. Amnesty International has consistently found its application to be racist, arbitrary and unfair. These findings have been demonstrated in more than 25 Amnesty International reports since 1987 alone, including *USA: The Death Penalty* (1987) and studies on Georgia (1995) and Texas (1998).

In 1994, Amnesty International called for a presidential commission to examine and report on the use of the death penalty in the USA, to allow informed discussion outside the highly charged political and emotional climate which has characterized the death penalty debate.[3] No such commission has been forthcoming.

---

[3] *USA: Open letter to the President on the death penalty*, AI Index: AMR 51/01/94, January 1994.

Public attitudes — brutalizing society

"This was very difficult for us. When I walked back into the jury room after delivering the verdict, I felt like a murderer."

Texas juror, 1998

The death penalty carries the official message that killing is an appropriate and effective response to killing. It is neither. It contributes to desensitizing the public to violence, and to increasing public tolerance for other human rights violations.

Executions were resumed in the USA in 1977. At first most lawmakers justified the death penalty on the grounds that it would prevent murder. However, its clear failure to deter crime any more effectively than other punishments has meant that deterrence is no longer advanced as a serious argument for the death penalty. In 1997 the Attorney General of Massachusetts said: "There is not a shred of credible evidence that the death penalty lowers the murder rate. In fact, without the death penalty the murder rate in Massachusetts is about half the national average. Maybe other states should be learning something from us." In Canada, between the abolition of the death penalty in 1976 and the end of 1995, the murder rate dropped by 34 per cent.

As a result, most politicians in the USA now speak not of deterrence, but of public demand for executions, of "victims' rights" and of retribution.

"Victim impact evidence" — in which relatives tell of their pain and suffering — can now be introduced at the sentencing phase in support of a prosecutor's call for the death penalty.[4] Such emotionally charged evidence often tips the outcome in favour of a death sentence.

The witnessing by relatives of the execution of their loved one's murderer has become routine, even encouraged. Relatives are regularly interviewed by the media, which often results in brutal messages associated with executions being taken further into society. In 1998 a family member told the press "If he [the murderer] could somehow die more painfully, that would be better... But I'll take what I can get."

There has been little research into the impact on jurors of deciding that a fellow human being will die. Anecdotal evidence suggests that many are traumatized by imposing a death sentence. For example, after a trial in 1998 in California, a distraught juror described recommending death as "...the hardest decision I've ever had to make in my life... no one should have to decide whether a person lives or dies."

---

[4] *Payne v. Tennessee* 1991.

The strain on the relatives of those on death row is immense, but their trauma is rarely recognized. For example, in Texas relatives of murder victims are offered counselling before and after witnessing the execution; the relatives of the executed prisoner are offered no such assistance.

Politicians claim that when the state kills killers, rather than compounding the brutality, it is helping the relatives of murder victims. In fact, relatives often report that the execution of the murderer does not help them come to terms with their loss. Indeed, the lengthy judicial proceedings in capital cases may only serve to prolong their suffering. In the absence of the death penalty, alternative punishments can be handed down far more quickly, allowing the healing process to begin sooner. A small but growing number of relatives of murder victims[5] in the USA are speaking out against the death penalty, arguing that it offers no solution to their personal tragedies.

Grief, anger and fear are natural responses to violent crime, but judicial and political officials must ensure that the law remains impartial and consistent with international standards. The rights of defendants must not be undermined by public or political desire for retribution.

The politics of death

"I cannot believe that to defend life and punish the person that kills, the State should in its turn kill. The death penalty is as inhuman as the crime which motivates it."

President Eduardo Frei of Chile, commuting a death sentence in 1996

The death penalty in the USA has become so highly politicized that virtually no politician is willing to speak out against it. Those who do are attacked as "soft on crime" by their opponents. When Governor Bill Clinton of Arkansas was campaigning for the US presidency in April 1992, he interrupted the campaign to return to Arkansas where he refused clemency for Ricky Ray Rector, a black mentally retarded death-row inmate. Ricky Rector's comprehension of his imminent execution was so limited that he left the dessert of his final meal as he wanted to "save it for later".

Many US politicians compete over who is "toughest" on criminals. A prospective Democratic candidate for governor in California launched his candidacy in late 1997 with a promise that, if elected, he would

---

[5] Some belong to the organization Murder Victims' Families for Reconciliation.

extend the use of the death penalty to include repeat child molesters and serial rapists. The incumbent Republican Governor of California had previously advocated the execution of children as young as 14. Both politicians were misleading the public since neither proposal was possible; the US Supreme Court had already ruled such measures unconstitutional.

© David Leeson /The Dallas Morning News

Demonstrators outside the prison where Karla Faye Tucker was executed in February 1998. Her killing demonstrated the death penalty's absolute denial of the possibility of human rehabilitation. Karla Faye Tucker was executed despite her acknowledged reform in prison; while on death row she educated herself and became deeply religious. She never denied her involvement in the murders for which she was sentenced to death and spoke about her desire to help others learn from her experience. Karla Faye Tucker is one of three women who have been executed in the USA since executions resumed in 1977. In June 1998 another 43 women remained on death row in 15 states.

Politicians are often critical of the time taken to complete the capital appeals process, thereby showing disdain for, and at the same time politicizing, the judicial process. In 1997, three months before elections, the Governor of New Jersey publicly demanded to know why none of the state's 14 death-row inmates had been executed. Her political opponent criticized her for waiting over three years before taking action, claiming that he "would take action on the death penalty from the first year" in office.

At the local level, the district attorney of the county where the crime occurs decides whether or not a particular murder should be prosecuted as a capital offence. This discretionary power, which may be influenced by political pressures or personal preference, has led to arbitrariness in the administration of the death penalty. For example, more than half of Pennsylvania's death sentences have been handed down in Philadelphia County, an area with only 14 per cent of the state's population. One of the 79 counties in Texas accounts for almost one-third of the state's death row; 132 of the state's 437 condemned prisoners were sentenced in Harris County.[6] In most states whose laws provide for the death penalty, district attorneys as well as judges are elected officials, some on party political lines. Thus both those who prosecute and those who adjudicate in capital trials may be vulnerable to political or electoral pressures. For example, in late 1994 the District Attorney of Oklahoma City campaigned for re-election on his record of having "sent 44 murderers to death row".

Human rights are supposed to be universal. Public support should never be used to justify a human rights violation. Yet in 1997, in a reply to Amnesty International, a member of the State Senate in Arkansas wrote: "If 77 per cent of Arkansas people want it [the death penalty], they will have it." The history of the USA is littered with examples of human rights abuses that had broad local support — including slavery, lynching and racial segregation — but which were abandoned after federal authorities had the courage to live up to universal legal and moral standards, and outlaw them.

Although opinion polls indicate that more than 70 per cent of the US public support the death penalty, that support is far less solid than it seems. It drops dramatically when alternatives, such as imprisonment without parole, are offered. Political leaders should not pander to public fears with inflammatory or false claims about the death penalty, but should instead encourage informed public debate.

---

[6] Figures as of January 1998.

Cruel, inhuman and degrading

"From hanging to electric chair to lethal injection: how much prettier can you make it? Yet the prettier it becomes, the uglier it is."

Scott Blystone, a Pennsylvania death row inmate, 1997

The cruelty of the death penalty is inescapable, regardless of the method used. Like torture, an execution constitutes an extreme physical and mental assault on a person already rendered helpless by the state and confined, sometimes for years, under the threat of death, often in harsh conditions.

Pedro Medina was executed in Florida's electric chair in 1997. Witnesses described how flames shot out of the facemask, causing officials to prematurely end the 2,000 volt charge. Florida's Attorney General seemed to boast of the malfunction, saying "People who wish to commit murder, they better not do it in the State of Florida because we may have a problem with our electric chair." Florida's Senate majority leader commented that: "A painless death is not a punishment."

The majority of states have abandoned electrocution and other older methods of execution — hanging, lethal gas and firing-squad — in favour of lethal injection, on the grounds that it is more "humane". Seventy of the 74 executions in 1997 were carried out by this method. However, lethal injection is not the clinical and painless process claimed by its proponents.

On the day of Tommie Smith's execution in Indiana in 1996, after searching for 16 minutes for a vein in Smith's arm (with Smith fully conscious) the execution team called in a doctor who tried unsuccess-

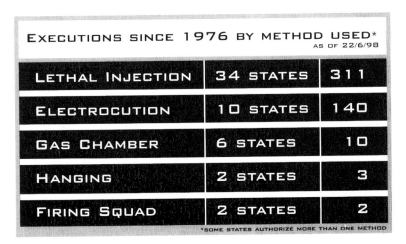

EXECUTIONS SINCE 1976 BY METHOD USED* AS OF 22/6/98		
LETHAL INJECTION	34 STATES	311
ELECTROCUTION	10 STATES	140
GAS CHAMBER	6 STATES	10
HANGING	2 STATES	3
FIRING SQUAD	2 STATES	2

*SOME STATES AUTHORIZE MORE THAN ONE METHOD

Death chamber and witness room, Southern Ohio Correctional Facility, Lucasville, Ohio. The 180 men currently facing execution in Ohio are given the choice between death by lethal injection, or electrocution.

fully to insert the needle into the prisoner's neck. After 36 minutes the team eventually injected the poison through a vein in his foot.

In 1996 Luis Mata was strapped down for execution where he remained for the next 70 minutes, with the needle inserted in his arm, while the Arizona Supreme Court heard legal arguments on his case. He lost. When the execution began, his head jerked back while his face convulsed. Minutes later, his chest and stomach began a series of quick, sharp spasms. Amnesty International has documented many other cases in which execution by lethal injection has resulted in prolonged deaths.

Race and the death penalty

"Even under the most sophisticated death penalty statutes, race continues to play a major role in determining who shall live and who shall die."

Justice Blackmun, US Supreme Court, 1994

The history of the death penalty in the USA shows that it has been applied in a racist manner and that any criminal justice system can be vulnerable to personal or social prejudice. In Virginia, for example, between 1908 and 1962, all those executed for rape were black, although only 55 per cent of those imprisoned for rape were black. Race continues to play a prominent role in virtually all aspects of the application of the death penalty in the USA.

The race of the murder victim appears to be a major factor in determining who is sentenced to death. Blacks and whites in the USA are the victims of murder in almost equal numbers, yet 82 per cent of prisoners executed since 1977 were convicted of the murder of a white person. In Kentucky, for example, every death sentence up to March 1996 was for the murder of a white victim, despite over 1,000 homicide victims in the state being black.[7] Nationwide, studies have consistently found that aggravating factors, such as the severity of the crime and the background of the defendant, cannot explain such disparities.

The race of the defendant is also a factor. A recent study, made public in June 1998, found that in Philadelphia the likelihood of receiving a death sentence is nearly four times higher if the defendant is black, after taking into account aggravating factors.[8] In effect, the study found that being black could in itself act as an aggravating factor in determining a sentence. Since Pennsylvania reintroduced the death penalty in 1978, the authorities in Philadelphia have sentenced to death more than eight times as many blacks as whites.

Nationwide, blacks are disproportionately represented on death row at both state and federal level. Blacks make up just 12 per cent of the country's population, but 42 per cent of the nation's condemned prisoners. In early 1998, of the 26 people under federal sentence of death (military and civilian), only five prisoners were white.

The overwhelming majority of district attorneys and other officials who make the decision as to whether to seek the death penalty are white. In 1998, of the 1,838 such officials in states with the death

---

[7] Thomas J. Keil and Gennaro F. Vito, University of Louisville, *Race and the Death Penalty in Kentucky Murder Trials: 1976 -1991*, in *American Journal of Criminal Justice*, Vol. 20 No. 1, 1995.

[8] The study was conducted by a leading expert on race and the death penalty in the USA, Professor David Baldus, together with statistician George Woodworth. Professor Baldus has also found evidence of race-of-victim disparities in over 30 states. In more than half of these states he has also found that the race of the defendant served as a predictor of who received a death sentence.

penalty, 22 were black, and 22 were Latino. The remainder were white.[9]

In many counties, black prospective jurors are disproportionately removed from the jury pool by prosecutors during jury selection. In Georgia, six of the 12 black prisoners executed since 1983 were convicted and sentenced by all-white juries after all black nominees had been removed. William Henry Hance was sentenced to death in 1984 by a jury where all but one black juror had been excluded by the prosecutor. Days before his execution in March 1994, that juror came forward to say that she had not voted for death but had been too intimidated to protest when her co-jurors said that the jury was unanimous. Another juror stated that several jurors had made racially derogatory comments about William Hance, referring to him as "one more sorry nigger that no one would miss".

During the trial of William Andrews in Utah in 1974, a note was found among the all-white jury depicting a hanging with the caption "Hang the Nigger's" (sic). Despite the fact that there was never any inquiry into how many of the jurors had seen or been involved in the drawing of the note, and what its impact was on their deliberations, William Andrews was executed in 1992. The Inter-American Commission on Human Rights concluded in 1996 that the USA had violated international standards on grounds including racial bias in the case.[10]

A 1986 Supreme Court ruling[11] that jurors could only be removed for "race neutral" reasons has failed to eliminate racial bias from jury selection. In 1987 the Assistant District Attorney for Philadelphia made a training video for the city's prosecutors. In the video he describes how to select a jury more likely to convict: "Let's face it, the blacks from low-income areas are less likely to convict. There's a resentment to law enforcement... You don't want those people on your jury... If you get a white teacher teaching in a black school who's sick of these guys, that may be the one to accept." The video also instructed trainee prosecutors on how to hide the racial motivation for their rejection of potential jurors. The tape did not become public until 1997.

In 1987, after reviewing a detailed statistical study which showed

---

[9] J. Pokorak, *Probing the Capital Prosecutor's Perspective: Race and Gender of the Discretionary Actors*, Cornell Law Review (forthcoming, 1998).

[10] Inter-American Commission on Human Rights, Report No. 57/96 (1998), Decision adopted 6 December 1996, published March 1998.

[11] *Batson v. Kentucky*.

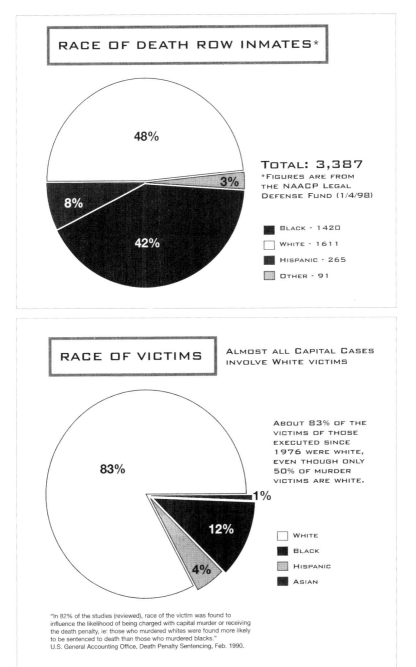

RACE OF DEATH ROW INMATES*

48%

3%

8%

42%

TOTAL: 3,387
*FIGURES ARE FROM
THE NAACP LEGAL
DEFENSE FUND (1/4/98)

- BLACK - 1420
- WHITE - 1611
- HISPANIC - 265
- OTHER - 91

RACE OF VICTIMS

ALMOST ALL CAPITAL CASES
INVOLVE WHITE VICTIMS

ABOUT 83% OF THE
VICTIMS OF THOSE
EXECUTED SINCE
1976 WERE WHITE,
EVEN THOUGH ONLY
50% OF MURDER
VICTIMS ARE WHITE.

83%

1%

12%

4%

- WHITE
- BLACK
- HISPANIC
- ASIAN

"In 82% of the studies (reviewed), race of the victim was found to
influence the likelihood of being charged with capital murder or receiving
the death penalty, ie: those who murdered whites were found more likely
to be sentenced to death than those who murdered blacks."
U.S. General Accounting Office, Death Penalty Sentencing, Feb. 1990.

that those who killed white victims in Georgia were four times more likely to be sentenced to death than other groups, and black defendants charged with killing white victims were the most likely group of all to receive the death penalty, the Supreme Court concluded that "apparent disparities in sentencing are an inevitable part of the criminal justice system" and that any system for determining guilt or punishment "has its weaknesses and potential for misuse". However, the Court ruled that the defendant, Warren McCleskey, had failed to prove that the decision-makers in his particular case had acted with discriminatory intent. In a dissenting opinion, Justice Brennan said that the "risk that race influenced McCleskey's sentence is intolerable by any imaginable standard". Warren McCleskey was executed in 1991.

In the late 1980s, following a request by the US Congress, the government's General Accounting Office (GAO) reviewed 28 studies on race and the death penalty. The GAO found that 82 per cent of them had revealed that "those who murdered whites [were] more likely to be sentenced to death than those who murdered blacks". Despite this evidence, an attempt to introduce a national Racial Justice Act, which would have allowed defendants to challenge their death sentence by producing statistical evidence of racial discrimination in the judicial process, failed in 1994. However, in 1998 Kentucky became the first state to pass this type of legislation.

Executing juvenile offenders

"Sentence of death shall not be imposed for crimes committed by persons below eighteen years of age."

Article 6(5), International Covenant on Civil and Political Rights

On 22 April 1998, Joseph John Cannon was led to the lethal injection chamber in Texas. The first attempt to kill him failed when the needle "blew out of his arm" as the lethal solution began to flow. Observers were led away while the needle was reinserted. Joseph John Cannon was 17 years old when he killed Anne Walsh, the crime for which he was sentenced to death. His life up to that point had been one of brutality and abuse. Despite being diagnosed as brain-damaged and schizophrenic, he received no treatment for his mental disorders. His childhood was so deprived that on death row he fared much better, learning to read and write.[12] His execution was

---

[12] See Amnesty International, *USA: The death penalty and juvenile offenders*, AI Index: AMR 51/23/91, October 1991. This report found that the large majority of juveniles on death row in the USA had suffered severely deprived, unstable or abusive family backgrounds.

a clear violation of international law which prohibits the execution of juvenile offenders.

On 18 May 1998, Texas again ignored international law when it executed Robert Anthony Carter for a crime he committed when he was 17. He too had been severely abused as a child, and had suffered brain damage, facts not made known to the jury which sentenced him to die. In May 1998, more than 25 other people were on death row in Texas for crimes they committed when under the age of 18. Elsewhere in the USA, more than 40 other such prisoners were under sentence of death.

International standards state that where the death penalty is retained, its scope must be strictly limited. One restriction recognizes that children have not yet reached a full understanding of their actions and bans the use of the death penalty against people who committed a capital crime when less than 18 years old. Yet the USA has executed eight juvenile offenders since 1990, more than any other country as far as Amnesty International is aware. Such executions are rare worldwide. Iran, Nigeria, Pakistan, Saudi Arabia and Yemen are the only other countries known to have executed juvenile offenders since 1990.

Sixteen-year-old Shareef Cousin became the USA's youngest death-row inmate when he was sentenced to death in 1996 in Louisiana. The prosecution's case hinged on the eye-witness testimony of a friend of the murdered man who told the jury she was "absolutely positive" Shareef Cousin was the murderer. After the trial Shareef Cousin's lawyers saw a copy of the original police statement in which she had said that she could not describe the assailant at all, because "it was dark, and I didn't have my contact [lenses] nor my glasses, so I'm coming at this at a disadvantage" and that she could see only "outlines and shapes and things". At his appeal in early 1998, Shareef Cousin won the right to a new trial.

UNITED STATES OF AMERICA

When the USA ratified the International Covenant on Civil and Political Rights (ICCPR) in 1992, it reserved the right to execute juvenile offenders. The UN Human Rights Committee has ruled that this reservation is incompatible with the object and purpose of the ICCPR and is therefore void. Whenever the USA sentences a juvenile offender to death it is breaking international law.[13] That such offenders are 30 or 40-year-olds when they come to be executed does not alter this fact. They are being killed for something they did when they were children.

Killing the mentally disabled

"Under Alabama law, you can't execute someone who is insane. You have to send him to an asylum, cure him up real good, then execute him."

Statement by the Assistant Attorney General of Alabama, who has since become a federal appeals court judge

International human rights standards ban the use of the death penalty against the insane and recommend that it be eliminated for people suffering from mental retardation or extremely limited mental competence.[14] These standards recognize that the death penalty is an inappropriate punishment for prisoners unable to fully understand the consequences of their actions or their punishment.

In 1986, the Supreme Court ruled that executing the "insane" is unconstitutional.[15] However, the ruling failed to specify procedures for determining whether a prisoner is insane, and offered little protection for those suffering severe mental health problems. For example, in mid-1998 California had scheduled the execution of Horace Kelly after a jury of lay people ruled that he was competent to be executed. There was overwhelming psychiatric evidence that Horace Kelly was severely mentally ill.

Varnall Weeks was diagnosed as being severely mentally ill and suffering from pervasive and bizarre religious delusions. An Alabama state judge acknowledged that Varnall Weeks suffered from paranoid schizophrenia. The ruling agreed that he was "insane" according to "the dictionary generic definition of insanity" and what "the average person on

---

[13] UN Human Rights Committee, UN Doc. CCPR/C/79/Add.50, para 1.4.

[14] UN Safeguards guaranteeing protection of the rights of those facing the death penalty: UN Economic and Social Council Resolution 1984/50; UN Economic and Social Council Resolution 1989/64, adopted 24 May 1989.

[15] *Ford v. Wainwright.*

the street would regard to be insane", but decided that his electrocution could proceed because he could answer a few questions, proving that he was legally "competent". He was executed in May 1995.

In 1989 the Supreme Court ruled that it was not unconstitutional for the death penalty to be used against mentally retarded defendants.[16] Some 30 prisoners suffering from mental disabilities have been executed since this ruling. The ruling indicated that the Supreme Court would reconsider the issue if there was evidence of a social consensus against the execution of the mentally retarded, and many states have made progress on this issue. In April 1998 Nebraska became the 12th state to adopt a law banning the execution of mentally retarded prisoners.

Death by omission

"I had always known, of course, that there were imperfections in the system, but I honestly thought that when a person faced death, he or she would at least be given adequate legal defense. I thought the Constitution promised that."

Sister Helen Prejean, *Dead Man Walking*

Whether a capital defendant lives or dies often depends more on their lawyer than their crime. Many defendants have been represented in court by attorneys lacking the skills, experience, resources or commitment to handle such complex cases. In contrast, they face prosecutors in an adversarial system who are often very experienced and highly motivated in their pursuit of a capital conviction.

International standards require states to ensure that all defendants who cannot afford to employ the lawyer of their choice "have a lawyer of experience and competence commensurate with the nature of the offence assigned to them in order to provide effective legal assistance, without payment by them if they lack sufficient means to pay for such services." Governments must provide sufficient funding and other resources to provide legal counsel for the poor and other disadvantaged people.[17]

In 1984, the Supreme Court ruled that errors by lawyers would not merit the reversal of the conviction or sentence unless the defendant could prove that such errors had prejudiced the outcome of the case, a standard of proof that is very difficult to meet.[18] The Court stated that:

[16] *Penry v. Lynaugh.*

[17] Principles 3 and 6 of the UN Basic Principles on the Role of Lawyers.

[18] *Strickland v. Washington.*

"the government is not responsible for, and hence not able to prevent, attorney errors". The result of this ruling has been that prisoners may have been executed as a result of mistakes by their lawyers.

Roger Coleman was represented at trial by lawyers who had never handled a murder case before. They failed to prepare adequately or to investigate evidence, including his alibi, and presented no mitigation. On appeal Roger Coleman was represented by volunteer lawyers unfamiliar with Virginia courts. They inadvertently filed the notice to appeal to the State Supreme Court one day late, and as a result the Court dismissed the appeal without a hearing. In 1991 the US Supreme Court ruled that Roger Coleman had lost his right to federal review because of his lawyers' mistake. Roger Coleman was executed in 1992 despite serious doubts about his guilt. In 1998 a Texas appeal court dismissed the appeal of LaRoyce Lathair Smith because his lawyer had filed it too late; one of the dissenting judges said that such a decision "borders on barbarism".

Calvin Burdine, who is openly homosexual, was sentenced to death in Texas after a trial at which he was represented by Joe Cannon. Joe Cannon, who at an earlier court hearing referred to homosexuals as "queers" and "fairies", did not object to a statement by the prosecutor that: "sending a homosexual to the penitentiary certainly isn't a very bad punishment for a homosexual". He also failed to exercise his right to remove three prospective jurors during jury selection who admitted to being prejudiced against homosexuals. Joe Cannon, who did not interview a single witness in preparing Calvin Burdine's defence, was seen to fall asleep repeatedly during the trial. However on appeal, the Texas Court of Criminal Appeals ruled that Calvin Burdine had failed to prove that this had affected the eventual outcome. Calvin Burdine, who has twice come within hours of execution, remains on death row.

On at least one occasion known to Amnesty International, a condemned prisoner has been forced to go to appeal without any lawyer at all. Exzavious Gibson, a Georgia death-row inmate with an IQ of between 76 and 81, was unrepresented at a state appeal hearing in late 1996. He had raised a claim that he had ineffective trial representation. When asked by the judge if he had any evidence in support of his claim, he stated: "I am not waiving any rights. I don't know what to plead." The Court denied the appeal. The rules of the appeal process mean that Exzavious Gibson's inability to raise issues at this hearing will have serious ramifications for him in later proceedings.

Death row, Kentucky State Penitentiary

Amnesty International has documented numerous other cases of inadequate legal representation for capital defendants. This problem has been exacerbated by two recent federal initiatives. In 1995 Congress voted to eliminate the federal funding for Post-Conviction Defender Organizations (PCDOs), which it had established in 1988 to provide legal aid to indigent death-row prisoners. In 1996, President Clinton signed the Anti-Terrorism and Effective Death Penalty Act into law. The Act, designed to reduce the time between sentence and execution, severely limits the appeals available to death row inmates in federal courts. Amnesty International believes that the Act dramatically increases the risk of wrongly convicted prisoners being executed.

Risk to the innocent

"We have enormous protection, the best by far, but we're never going to have a system that will never execute an innocent person."
Chair of the US House of Representatives Judiciary Committee,
supporting the death penalty, 1997

For many people, the risk of executing an innocent prisoner is reason enough to abandon the death penalty. No criminal justice system is immune from mistakes, especially in the tense climate that prevails after brutal crimes are committed. Where legal representation is inadequate, or punishment is driven by a desire for retribution, or distorted by racial prejudice, the risk of fatal error increases. US legal safeguards, several of which have been eroded in the recent past, have manifestly failed to prevent major errors in some cases. At least 75 wrongly convicted people have been released from death row since 1973. Yet US politicians either continue to deny the possibility of executing an innocent person, or seem willing to accept it as the price for retaining the death penalty.

Leonel Herrera was executed in Texas after the US Supreme Court denied his appeal despite newly discovered evidence that appeared to show he was innocent.[19] The Court ruled that there was no constitutional right to federal intervention because of new evidence where the original trial had been free from procedural error. In a strongly worded dissent, three justices argued that the Constitution's protection against cruel and unusual punishments did not end once a defendant had been sentenced to death, and that "[t]he execution of a person who can show that he is innocent comes perilously close to simple murder".

---

[19] *Herrera v. Collins*, 1993.

The Supreme Court evaded its responsibility by pointing out that Leonel Herrera could take his claim of innocence to the Texas Board of Pardons and Paroles. Since Texas resumed executions in 1982 the Board has, to Amnesty International's knowledge, met only once to consider the commutation of a death sentence. More than 150 executions have been carried out in Texas during that time; in some cases there were still doubts over the prisoner's guilt. Leonel Herrera was executed in 1993 after the Board refused to convene a clemency hearing to review the new evidence of his innocence. The Board made its only recommendation for commutation in June 1998 in the case of Henry Lee Lucas, who was facing imminent execution despite former and current Texas Attorneys General stating that it was highly improbable that he had committed the crime for which he had been sentenced to death in 1984. While several prisoners in other states have been granted clemency on the grounds of possible innocence, it remains extremely rare.

Curtis Kyles was released and charges against him were dropped in 1997 after he had been subjected to five capital trials in Louisiana. He was held in prison for 14 years, twice coming close to execution. In 1995 the US Supreme Court ruled that the verdict was unsafe because the prosecution

© Loren Santow/Impact Visuals

Perry Cobb (above) and Gary Gauger: two of those released from death row after having their convictions quashed. More than 70 other people have been wrongly convicted and sentenced to death before finally being released. Some had come close to execution. No one knows how many innocent people have been sent to their death.

© AI

119

had withheld crucial evidence about the unreliability of eye-witness testimony along with important information about a paid informant who may have been the actual murderer.

Around one per cent of those sentenced to death since 1972 have later been found innocent. Many have come within hours of execution. Politicians have claimed that such releases are the sign of a justice system working. This not only ignores the unique suffering of a person condemned to death, but also denies the fact that in most cases innocence was only proved after the work of a few dedicated individuals, usually working for little or no pay. Many of the 75 released prisoners were spared only because of the intervention of attorneys from PCDOs. With the withdrawal of their federal funding, most of these resource centres have now been forced to close.

No one knows how many prisoners have been executed in the USA for crimes they did not commit. Amnesty International has documented numerous cases of people who went to their deaths despite serious doubts about their guilt.

National and international concern

Several national and international organizations not opposed in principle to the death penalty have called for a moratorium on executions in the USA because of the way the death penalty is being applied. In 1997, the American Bar Association (ABA) called for an immediate moratorium until the procedures used in capital cases meet basic principles of fairness and reliability. Other bar associations have followed the ABA's example at a local level.

In late 1997, the UN Special Rapporteur on extrajudicial, summary or arbitrary executions visited the USA to investigate its use of the death penalty. In his report, the Special Rapporteur called for a moratorium on executions in the USA.[20] He concluded, among other things, that "race, ethnic origin and economic status appear to be key determinants of who will, and who will not, receive a death sentence".

In 1996 the International Commission of Jurists concluded that "the administration of the death penalty in the United States will remain arbitrary, and racially discriminatory, and prospects of a fair hearing for capital offenders cannot (and will not) be assured" without substantial remedial measures.[21] No such measures have been put into effect.

[20] UN Doc. E/CN.4/1998/68/Add.3., 22 January 1998, para. 148.

[21] *Administration of the death penalty in the United States. Report of a Mission,* June 1996.

CHAPTER 6

Official responses

"The rights to life and dignity are the most important of all human rights... And this must be demonstrated by the State in everything that it does, including the way it punishes criminals."

Justice Chaskalson, South African Constitutional Court, 1995

The legislators who designed the current death penalty statutes in the USA did so to punish the most heinous crimes with the "ultimate" punishment. Years later, the death penalty in the USA is often enacted in vengeance, applied in an arbitrary manner, subject to bias because of the defendant's race or economic status, or driven by the political ambitions of those who impose it.

In replies to Amnesty International, the federal authorities have refused to answer these concerns in any detail. They state their support for the death penalty "in appropriate cases". Despite the overwhelming evidence to the contrary, they assert that they are "unalterably opposed to its application in an unfair manner, particularly if that unfairness is grounded in racial or other discrimination", and that the Supreme Court provides adequate safeguards.

The federal government has repeatedly refused to intervene on the death penalty on the grounds that it is solely a matter for the individual states concerned and the federal appeal courts. This approach is an abdication of its international obligations to ensure fairness and non-discrimination in the judicial system. In his 1998 report, the UN Special Rapporteur on extrajudicial, summary or arbitrary executions said that "the Federal Government cannot claim to represent the states at the international level and at the same time fail to take steps to implement international obligations accepted on their behalf."[22]

Recommendations

The death penalty is a violation of human rights, rights that belong to every human being, even those convicted of serious crimes. In the USA its application is arbitrary, unfair and prone to racial bias.

1. The US government and all state authorities whose laws provide for capital punishment should abolish the death penalty for all crimes.

2. Pending abolition, the US federal and state governments should impose an immediate moratorium on executions.

[22] UN Doc. E/CN.4/1998/68/Add.3, 22 January 1998, para.142.

UNITED STATES OF AMERICA

3. The 24 states that allow for the use of the death penalty for crimes committed under the age of 18 should raise the minimum age to 18. The US government should withdraw its reservation to Article 6(5) of the International Covenant on Civil and Political Rights.

4. All states which allow the use of the death penalty against mentally impaired defendants should enact legislation to prevent this practice.

5. The federal and state authorities should ensure that capital defendants are represented by attorneys who are adequately trained and resourced, and experienced in the complexities of capital proceedings.

7

DOUBLE STANDARDS:

The USA and international human rights protection

"We have an obligation that we must meet, as members of organizations we helped build, to abide by rules we helped write, to further goals of law, peace and prosperity that Americans deeply support."

US Secretary of State Madeleine Albright, January 1998

The international system of human rights protection built over the past 50 years is based on the understanding not only that human rights are universal, but that they transcend the sovereignty of individual states. Despite the USA's leading role in establishing this system, it has been reluctant to submit itself to international human rights law and to accept the same minimum standards for its own conduct that it demands from other countries.

The USA has avoided scrutiny by UN and Inter-American bodies set up to protect human rights by refusing to recognize their right to hear complaints from people in the USA. It has been slow to agree to international human rights standards and has still not ratified several important treaties. When it has ratified human rights treaties, it has reserved the right to ignore some of their provisions, undermining the protection they offer.

Amnesty International believes that all countries, including the USA, should accept the primacy of international law. The USA should adjust its legislation to conform with international human rights standards. It should ratify without reservations all human rights treaties and withdraw existing reservations that undermine its international commitments and the effectiveness of international human rights law.

A troubled history

The USA played a fundamental role in the creation of the UN and the drafting of the Universal Declaration of Human Rights. Within the UN it holds a privileged position, being one of five permanent members of the Security Council with the right of veto, giving it the power to block decisions. Over the decades, the USA has participated in numerous conferences and forums where international human rights standards have been drafted and adopted by the world's governments.

The USA played an equally important role in the establishment of regional organizations such as the Organization of American States (OAS), the Organization for Security and Co-operation in Europe (OSCE), the North Atlantic Treaty Organization (NATO) and the Asia - Pacific Economic Co-operation (APEC). Apart from APEC, these organizations emerged during the Cold War in response to the perceived threat from the Soviet bloc. Over the past 15 years the geopolitical landscape has been transformed and some of these organizations have substantially developed the human rights dimension of their work.

At the UN and within regional bodies, the USA has repeatedly stressed the importance of the principles of international law and human rights. However, its relationship with intergovernmental organizations such as the UN has been marked by deep distrust and a lack of practical cooperation. This can be seen in the USA's failure to pay its dues to the UN, building up arrears of over a billion dollars. It is also reflected in the USA's position in intergovernmental efforts to create a permanent International Criminal Court to try perpetrators of crimes against humanity when states are unwilling or unable to do so. The USA has advocated positions that would threaten the independence of the court and undermine its effectiveness and credibility.

The use, and abuse, of international law by the USA has taken many forms in recent decades. For example, in 1979 the USA filed a suit against Iran before the International Court of Justice (International Court) for taking US diplomats hostage in Tehran. Yet four years later, the USA refused to recognize the jurisdiction of the International Court when Nicaragua denounced US-sponsored military and paramilitary activity against the Sandinista government which led to serious human rights abuses. The USA subsequently used its power of veto to prevent the UN Security Council taking action to implement the International Court's 1986 ruling on the Nicaraguan case. (Iran is the only other state not to have respected an International Court ruling.)

Another example of the USA ignoring international law was the abduction from Mexico of a Mexican citizen by agents paid by, and under the orders of, a US government agency in 1990. Humberto Álvarez Macháin was wanted in the USA for kidnapping and killing a Drug Enforcement Agency (DEA) agent. The DEA abducted Álvarez

Machaín from Mexico, although he could legally have been brought to court in the USA under an extradition treaty. The abduction was endorsed by the Supreme Court.[1] The UN Working Group on Arbitrary Detention declared that the abduction was an arbitrary detention and constituted illegitimate interference by one state in the sovereignty of another; it was therefore a violation of international law.[2]

Ángel Francisco Breard, executed in flagrant defiance of international law.

© HO/Reuters

Paraguayan citizen Ángel Francisco Breard was executed in 1998 despite an International Court of Justice order that his execution should be suspended. Under the Vienna Convention on Consular Relations, to which the USA is party, Ángel Francisco Breard had the right to assistance from Paraguayan consular officials — assistance which he had been denied. Paraguay took his case to the International Court on the grounds that the Vienna Convention on Consular Relations had been violated. On 9 April 1998 the International Court ordered the execution to be suspended until it had considered the case — a decision that was binding on the USA under international law. Five days later, in flagrant defiance of the International Court's decision, the state authorities in Virginia executed Ángel Francisco Breard.

---

[1] US Supreme Court ruling, 15 June 1992, in the case of Álvarez Machaín.

[2] UN Doc: E/CN.4/1994/27, Decision No. 48/1993 (USA).

National versus international standards: false division

"It's an appalling intrusion by the UN... there's only one court that matters here. That's the US Supreme Court. There's only one law that applies. That's the US Constitution."

A spokesperson for Senator Jesse Helms,
Chairman of the Senate Foreign Relations Committee, 1998

Successive US administrations have challenged the primacy of international human rights law, in effect arguing that the human rights standards used to measure other countries' conduct do not apply to the USA.

One argument put forward is that the US legal system already contains an unsurpassable system of guarantees based on the Constitution and the decisions of the Supreme Court. The additional protection offered by international standards is regarded as superfluous.[3] Certainly the Bill of Rights was a remarkable breakthrough in establishing fundamental rights and freedoms, a breakthrough which the US judicial system has elaborated and defended. However, human rights standards have evolved, and today the level of human rights protection recognized in US law falls short of some of the minimum standards set down in human rights treaties. Important internationally recognized rights and standards are not always reflected in domestic US law — such as the ban on using the death penalty against juvenile offenders.

Another argument is that under the US legal system international treaties are inferior in status to the Constitution. The system puts international treaties on a par with federal laws, and in case of conflict between the two sources of law, the most recent prevails. According to this position, the USA could invoke domestic law to justify noncompliance with international obligations — a breach of international legal principles. The principle that states may not invoke internal laws to avoid complying with their commitments under international treaties is expressly provided by the Vienna Convention on the Law of Treaties. (The USA signed the Vienna Convention on the Law of Treaties in 1970, but has not yet ratified it.)

---

[3] This was one of the arguments used by the USA in its initial report to the UN Human Rights Committee in 1994 to justify its reservation to the ICCPR. UN Doc: CCPR/C/81/Add.4, paras 7 and 8.

In a direct challenge to the status of international law, the USA has on several occasions claimed that the American Declaration on the Rights and Duties of Man[4] is not binding on the USA, even though the Inter-American Court of Human Rights[5] and the Inter-American Commission on Human Rights have considered the Declaration part of customary law binding on all member states of the OAS.

The federal system has also been used to justify evasion of international commitments. Irineo Tristán Montoya, a Mexican citizen, was executed in June 1997. He had been sentenced to death in 1986 by a Texas court without the consular assistance guaranteed by the Vienna Convention on Consular Relations. He had been subjected to a lengthy interrogation without a lawyer and had signed a confession in English, a language he did not read, speak or understand. He was charged as an accessory to murder and sentenced to death; the actual killer received a prison sentence.[6] After the execution, the governor of Texas stated that Texas had not signed this Convention and was therefore not bound by it. This runs directly counter to the long-standing principle of international law that the state is the subject of international law, regardless of whether its system is unitary, decentralized or federal, and is responsible for ensuring that all government authorities in the country abide by international law. The US Constitution expressly establishes that powers to sign and ratify treaties reside with the federal state and not with the individual states.

Reaction to other governments

The USA's reaction within intergovernmental organizations such as the UN to human rights violations by other governments has been selective and partial. Officials have criticized countries considered hostile, but have been unwilling to take appropriate action when abuses are committed by US allies or when action would run counter to the USA's

---

[4] For example, in cases of human rights violations presented to the Inter-American Commission on Human Rights, the USA claimed that the American Declaration was not binding on the USA. (IACHR Case No. 2141/ Resolution 23/8 and No. 9647/ Resolution No.3/87)

[5] Inter-American Court of Human Rights, Advisory Opinion OC 10/89, 14 July 1989.

[6] In a similar case Mario Murphy, also a Mexican citizen, was executed in 1997. He was the only one of six people involved in a 1991 murder in Virginia to receive a death sentence. The others, all US citizens, were offered plea bargains and received prison terms.

political or economic interests. The USA is, of course, not alone in this selective approach, but its actions seem to suggest that international law and inter-governmental systems are instruments for advancing its own interests, willingly taken up when they serve to legitimize or implement its foreign policy but discarded and even condemned when seen as an obstacle or as irrelevant to these interests.

Examples include the US government's long-standing refusal to criticize blatant human rights violations by Israel against the Palestinian population; its passivity in the face of gross human rights violations in Saudi Arabia; and its willingness to ignore for many crucial months in 1996 and 1997 massive human rights abuses committed against civilians and refugees by the armed opposition in Zaire, now the Democratic Republic of the Congo (DRC). Until recently the USA failed to effectively oppose the obstruction of UN investigation missions by the DRC authorities. US government officials have denied, ignored or played down massacres of unarmed civilians in Rwanda by members of the army since 1994.

One of the clearest examples of the USA's changing attitude to human rights violations in different circumstances is that of Iraq. During the 1980s Iraqi forces committed gross and widespread abuses, including repeated massacres of Kurdish civilians, many of them children, sometimes using chemical weapons. Amnesty International repeatedly appealed for action, yet neither the US authorities nor the UN responded. However, after Iraq invaded Kuwait in August 1990, the US attitude changed dramatically. The USA repeatedly cited the Iraqi government's appalling human rights record to gather support for UN military intervention in the Gulf.

Human rights treaties: unwilling party

There are only two countries in the world that have not ratified the Convention on the Rights of the Child. One is the collapsed state of Somalia which has no recognized government — the other is the USA. Despite the strength and achievements of the US women's movement, the USA is also one of only a handful of countries that have not ratified the Convention on the Elimination of All Forms of Discrimination against Women.

The USA's resistance to international human rights commitments is demonstrated by its delays in ratifying human rights treaties and its use of reservations to undermine a treaty's full protection.

The first UN human rights treaty ratified by the USA was the

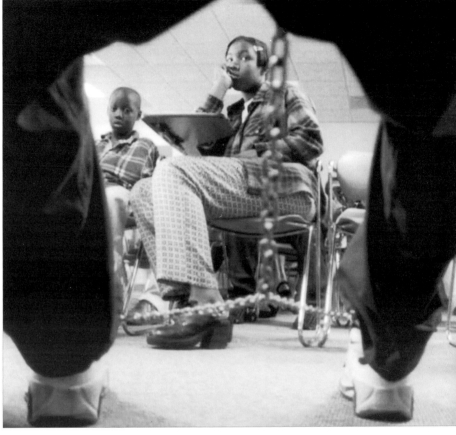

A juvenile held in leg-irons in breach of international standards. The USA is one of only two countries in the world that have not yet ratified the UN Convention on the Rights of the Child.

Convention on the Prevention and Punishment of the Crime of Genocide. It ratified the Convention in 1988, 40 years after signing it and after 97 other states had already ratified it. The USA took 28 years to ratify the International Convention on the Elimination of All Forms of Racial Discrimination[7], after 133 other states had already ratified it. At least 71 other states ratified the Convention against Torture[8] before the USA.

[7] The USA signed the Convention on 28 September 1966 and ratified it on 21 October 1994.

[8] The USA signed the Convention against Torture on 18 April 1988 and ratified it on 21 October 1994.

UNITED STATES OF AMERICA

It was only in 1992, after 109 other states, that the USA ratified the International Covenant on Civil and Political Rights (ICCPR), 26 years after its adoption by the UN General Assembly.[9] The ICCPR is one of two principal treaties protecting human rights as enshrined in the Universal Declaration of Human Rights. The other — the International Covenant on Economic, Social and Cultural Rights — has still not been ratified by the USA, although it signed it in 1977.

The USA's reluctance to support international human rights protection mechanisms is even more marked in the inter-American system. The USA has long been a leading member of the OAS. It participated in the Ninth International Conference of American States in Bogotá, Colombia, in 1948, at which the OAS Charter was adopted, and helped construct the inter-American system, in particular its political-diplomatic and military components.

Yet the USA has refused to recognize any regional human rights treaties: it has not ratified the American Convention on Human Rights, adopted by the OAS in 1969, and has not even signed the Inter-American Convention to Prevent and Punish Torture, the Inter-American Convention on Forced Disappearance of Persons and the Inter-American Convention to Prevent, Punish and Eradicate Violence against Women.

Undermining treaty protection

When it has ratified human rights treaties, the USA has consistently diluted their force by making reservations, interpretations and statements which have limited the protection they offer.

The USA has declared that it will apply the ICCPR and the Convention against Torture only to the extent that domestic law allows, effectively rendering the treaties meaningless as a means of strengthening human rights protection.

The USA has made numerous reservations to the ICCPR (particularly Articles 6 and 7), some of which are contrary to the object and aims of the treaty. For example, Article 6.5 of the Covenant prohibits passing a death sentence on anyone aged less than 18 at the time of the crime. This is deemed such a fundamental safeguard that it may never be suspended, even in times of war or internal conflict.[10] Yet the USA has

---

[9] The USA signed the ICCPR on 5 October 1977.

[10] Additional Protocols I and II to the Geneva Conventions of 12 August 1949 relating to the protection of victims of armed conflict not of an international character, articles 77.5 and 6.4 respectively.

entered a reservation insisting on its right to execute juvenile offenders.

Another example is a reservation to the right to freedom from cruel, inhuman or degrading treatment or punishment in the ICCPR. The USA allows the continued use of corporal punishment in schools[11] and the imposition of certain conditions of detention (such as prolonged solitary confinement) considered in international human rights practice as forms of torture or cruel treatment.

The Human Rights Committee, the UN body of experts that monitors states' compliance with the ICCPR, has stated that several of these reservations are incompatible with international law. In 1995 it recommended that the USA consider withdrawing them, in particular those relating to the death penalty and to the right not to be tortured.[12]

There are other areas where reservations deny people in the USA the protection to which they should be entitled.[13] These include allowing male guards to staff women's prisons; interference in the private lives of people in those states which consider sexual relations between consenting adults of the same sex to be a crime; the nomination system in some states for judges, affecting the right to an independent and impartial tribunal[14]; and the indefinite detention and lack of procedural safeguards for foreign nationals facing expulsion or extradition.

Despite its role in developing international human rights law, the USA has sometimes stood in the way of developing new standards, for example with regard to child soldiers, the International Criminal Court and landmines. The USA has repeatedly blocked the adoption of an Optional Protocol to the Convention on the Rights of the Child, which would prohibit the recruitment of people under the age of 18 into armed forces and their participation in hostilities. The US position is ironic given that the protocol could only be ratified by states which are party

---

[11] UN Human Rights Committee, General Comment No. 21, para. 5, UN Doc: HRI/GEN/1/Rev.3.

[12] UN Human Rights Committee, General Comment No. 24, and UN Doc: CCPR/C/79/Add.50, 7 April 1995.

[13] See UN Doc: CCPR/C/79/Add.50, Human Rights Committee.

[14] In some US states, judges are elected, in others they are nominated by the governor or other judges. In some states, legal training is not a prerequisite in order to be a judge. In many states judicial appointment systems fall short of the UN Basic Principles on the Independence of the Judiciary. In 1995 the UN Human Rights Committee expressed concern about this, and about the fact that "in many rural areas justice is administered by unqualified and untrained persons". UN Doc: CCPR/C/79/Add.50, para. 23.

to the Convention on the Rights of the Child (which the USA is not), and, moreover, would be optional.

Avoiding scrutiny

The USA has avoided scrutiny by international human rights protection bodies for many years, although recently it has become somewhat more open. In 1994 the USA presented its first report on implementation of the ICCPR to the Human Rights Committee. Similarly, it agreed to a request by the UN Working Group on Arbitrary Detention to visit the Guantanamo naval base in 1995, although the visit did not take place for various reasons. However, the USA has yet to present its initial report to the Committee against Torture, due since November 1995, as well as two reports on implementation of the International Convention on the Elimination of All Forms of Racial Discrimination, overdue since November 1995 and November 1997.

The USA has not recognized the jurisdiction of the Human Rights Committee and the Committee against Torture to hear individuals' complaints that their rights have been violated under the ICCPR and the Convention against Torture. People in the USA are therefore denied the possibility of recourse to these international protection mechanisms. In addition, they do not have the protection offered by the American Convention on Human Rights through the Inter-American Commission on Human Rights and the Inter-American Court of Human Rights. By contrast, 93 countries allow the Human Rights Committee to hear individual complaints and 39 allow individual recourse to the Committee against Torture.[15]

Human rights experts appointed by the UN Commission on Human Rights to investigate particular types of human rights abuse have not received full cooperation from the US authorities. One such expert, the UN Special Rapporteur on extrajudicial, summary or arbitrary executions, was able to visit the USA only in late 1997, having repeatedly sought access since 1994. Much of the information he requested was not provided and he faced obstacles in meeting senior federal officials. His report to the Commission on Human Rights questioned the federal government's commitment to enforcing international obligations at home.[16] The response of many US politicians was hostile: Republican National Committee Chairman Jim Nicholson said "I call on the Clinton administration and UN ambassador Bill Richardson to clearly and publicly

---

[15] As of 1 January 1998, UN Doc: E/CN.4/1998/36, rev.1.

[16] UN Doc: E/CN.4/1998/68/Add.3, 22 January 1998, para. 144.

renounce this report, and not one dime of the so-called 'US arrearage' should be paid until the report is withdrawn and apologized for."

Other UN human rights experts have visited the USA, but their recommendations to the government have frequently not been implemented. For example, the Special Rapporteur on the sale of children, child prostitution and child pornography visited the USA in 1996. Her recommendations included ratification of the Convention on the Rights of the Child and the establishment of a Children's Ombudsman, but these steps have yet to be taken.

It is a paradox that the nation that did so much to articulate and codify human rights in its foundation documents has so consistently resisted the effective functioning of an international framework to protect these principles and values.

Recommendations

In order to live up to its stated commitment to universal human rights, the USA should:

1. Ratify, without reservations, human rights treaties that it has not yet ratified, in particular the Convention on the Rights of the Child, the Convention on the Elimination of All Forms of Discrimination against Women, the International Covenant on Economic, Social and Cultural Rights, the Convention relating to the status of refugees, the American Convention on Human Rights and other Inter-American human rights treaties.

2. Withdraw its reservations to the International Covenant on Civil and Political Rights and the Convention Against Torture, in particular those that restrict the implementation of Articles 6 and 7 of the International Covenant on Civil and Political Rights and Articles 1, 3 and 16 of the Convention against Torture. It should also withdraw reservations that restrict the USA's fulfilment of international obligations in its domestic law.

3. Ratify the (first) Optional Protocol to the International Covenant on Civil and Political Rights (allowing the right of individual petition to the Human Rights Committee) and recognize the competence of the Committee against Torture to receive and act on individual cases; on ratification of the American Convention on Human Rights, recognize the competence of the Inter-American Court of Human Rights.

4. Submit to the Committee against Torture the USA's initial report on

its implementation of the Convention against Torture, which was due in November 1995.

5. Support an Optional Protocol to the Convention on the Rights of the Child which prohibits the recruitment of people under 18 years of age into governmental or non-governmental armed forces and their participation in hostilities.

© UN Photo 185522/A. Brizzi

The UN building in New York

8

OUT OF CONTROL: US arms and human rights abuses

"I had electric shocks applied to my feet and hands for so long they had to change the batteries, and I became so weak I told them what they wanted."

Pius Lustrilanang, an Indonesian political activist speaking in February 1998, describing his torture with an electro-shock stun gun.

US companies were the first to develop stun guns for use against human beings and are among the world's leading suppliers. The US government keeps export data on such equipment secret, but in 1998 Amnesty International found leaked government documents showing that the US Commerce Department had licensed the export of thousands of stun guns to Indonesia in 1993, in the face of persistent reports of electro-shock torture by Indonesian government agents.

The US government's claim to promote human rights and freedom around the globe is undermined by its support for armed forces known to commit human rights abuses. The USA has supplied arms, security equipment and training to governments and armed groups that have committed torture, political killings and other human rights abuses in countries around the world. Oversight by public bodies remains inadequate to the task of ensuring that US supplies do not contribute to further human rights violations.

The USA dominates the post-Cold War global market for arms and security equipment. It is estimated that from 1989 to 1996 the USA sold more than $117 billion of arms, about 45 per cent of the global total. Sales are often supported by official financial assistance, military training and logistical support programs. Successive US governments have authorized exports to recipients with a record of human rights abuse, and have failed to publish comprehensive and timely information on the export of US small arms and law enforcement equipment — the most common tools of human rights abuse.

Amnesty International believes that the USA should adopt and rigorously enforce a Code of Conduct to regulate all military, security and police sales and assistance to other countries, in order to ensure that US transfers of such equipment or expertise do not contribute to serious human rights abuses elsewhere. It should publish more information and strengthen the monitoring of end users. The USA should ban outright the export of equipment solely used for executions or torture, and suspend exports of equipment that inherently lends itself to human rights abuse.

Tackling the deadly trade

Turkey is an example of how US arms have been misused to commit serious human rights violations, as well as the obstacles facing efforts to challenge this. Amnesty International questioned the US government about the use of US military helicopters and US armoured vehicles for human rights violations in early 1995.[1] Under pressure from Congress, the State Department compiled a report issued in June 1995 on human rights violations by the Turkish military which concluded that there was "highly credible" evidence that US-supplied helicopters, armoured personnel carriers, trucks and jet fighters had been used in some village evacuations involving human rights violations.[2] The US government committed itself to "sustained discussion" with Turkish authorities "on the issue of human rights".

Following the submission of more detailed evidence on human rights violations carried out with US military equipment,[3] the US government temporarily suspended the sale of advanced attack helicopters and other equipment in 1996. Responding to further pressure from Congress, another State Department report on the use of US military equipment was issued in July 1997. This admitted that Turkey's special units of paramilitary gendarmes and police — two of the forces most frequently accused of political killings, "disappearances" and torture — were using M-16 and AR-15S assault rifles, M-203 grenade launchers and helicopters obtained from the USA.[4]

---

[1] See for example, Amnesty International, *Turkey: A policy of denial*, 1995. (AI Index: EUR 44/01/95).

[2] US State Department, *Report on Allegations of Human Rights Abuses by the Turkish Military and on the Situation in Cyprus*, June 1995.

[3] See for example, Amnesty International, *Turkey: No security without human rights*, 1996, (AI Index: EUR/44/84/96), and Human Rights Watch, *Weapons Transfers and the Violations of the Laws of War in Turkey*, 1995.

[4] US State Department, *Report on US Military Equipment and Human Rights Violations in Turkey*, July 1997.

The US government held up a few US arms exports to Turkey in 1997, where reported abuses by the Turkish security forces have persisted, albeit at a lower level. But in 1998 it was reported that the export of hundreds more US armoured vehicles had been allowed, and that the US Defense Secretary had visited Turkey and lobbied on behalf of US companies wishing to co-produce advanced attack helicopters there. In April 1998, a US company was negotiating to sell 10,000 electro-shock weapons to the Turkish police, despite its long-standing and documented record of practising electro-shock torture. At the same time, a Turkish Parliamentary Commission of Human Rights delegation announced that it had discovered disturbing evidence of torture — including electrical equipment designed for torture — when allowed a rare inspection of police interrogation centres in eastern and southeastern Turkey.

Lack of transparency

Although successive US governments have published more information on arms transfers than most other significant arms exporting states, official information on the export of US small arms and security equipment and services has been sparse or non-existent.

Light weapons

Small arms have been the principal weapons used to commit human rights abuses in the world's many internal armed conflicts during the 1990s, where more than 80 per cent of casualties have been civilians, mostly women and children. Yet there is a glaring loophole in Congressional and public scrutiny of US small arms exports:[5] the Arms Export Control Act requires advanced notice to be given to Congress only for arms sales of $14 million or more. Many small arms sales fall below this amount.

In September 1997 the US government released, for the first time since 1981, detailed statistics on military equipment export authorizations.[6] This showed that US arms exports worldwide had grown rapidly. It also showed that the USA had granted export licences for rifles, small

---

[5] See Lora Lumpe, *The Evolution of US Policy on Small/Light Arms Exports*, draft provided by the author, December 1997.

[6] See US State Department and US Department of Defense, *Foreign Military Assistance Act, Report to Congress, Financial Year 1996: Authorized US Commercial Exports, Military Assistance, Foreign Military Sales and Military Imports*, September 1997. By mid-1998, the US government had published no more recent data on small arms exports.

arms, pistols, revolvers, ammunition, guns, grenades and riot control chemical weapons to countries where human rights violations were severe and persistent, including Bahrain, Bolivia, Colombia, Egypt, Israel, Mexico, Pakistan, Saudi Arabia and Turkey.

At the time that export licences were being granted to send 47,022 "chemical agents" and 35,844 "pistols and revolvers" to Bahrain, the US State Department was recording that "On a regular basis, from January through to July, the security forces used tear gas, rubber bullets and, occasionally, live ammunition to disperse gatherings during which protestors called for the establishment of an elected parliament."[7]

Anti-personnel mines, which have inherently indiscriminate effects, have resulted in innumerable civilian deaths and injuries. In 1994, the US President was the first world leader to call for their "eventual elimination", but the US government refused to sign the Convention on the Prohibition of the Use, Stockpiling, Production and Transfer of Anti-Personnel Mines and on Their Destruction (the Ottawa Convention). This Convention was signed by 122 states in Ottawa in December 1997. The governments of China, Egypt, India, Israel, North Korea, Pakistan, Russia and South Korea joined the USA in refusing to sign.

Law enforcement equipment

Exports of law enforcement equipment from the USA include items such as handcuffs and tear-gas sprays, and other riot control equipment, but almost no official information is published about this trade. Some items used in the USA and exported, such as leg-irons, thumb-cuffs, electro-shock weapons and OC (pepper) spray, easily or inherently lend themselves to torture, ill-treatment or excessive force. The US government has stated that human rights considerations should be taken into account when making licensing decisions. However, procedures to curb exports of such equipment are grossly inadequate.

There is no requirement to provide prior notification of proposed exports to Congress and no requirement to publish meaningful, detailed data on a regular basis. However, using the US Freedom of Information Act, the Federation of American Scientists showed that from September 1991 to December 1993 the US Commerce Department had issued over 350 export licences worth more than $27 million for: "saps[8], thumb-cuffs, thumb-screws, leg-irons, shackles and handcuffs; *specially designed implements of torture* [emphasis added]; strait jackets, plastic

---

[7] US State Department, *Bahrain Country Report on Human Rights Practices for 1996.*

[8] A reinforced or weighted glove.

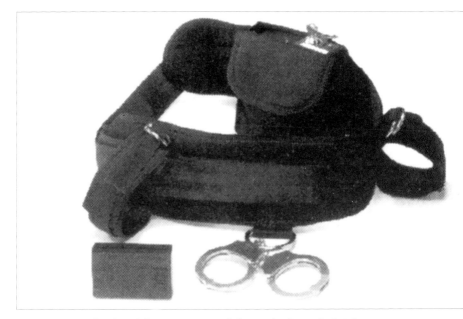

A US company developed this remote control electro-shock stun belt. When worn by a suspect or prisoner powerful electro-shocks can be inflicted by the officer or prison guard. In 1997 a US-supplied remote control electro-shock belt was being tested in a prison in South Africa, a country with persistent problems of torture and ill-treatment by members of the security forces.

handcuffs, police helmets and shields". These were issued for 57 countries, many of them with poor human rights records. In addition, over 2,000 licences were issued for 105 countries under another export category, which combined electro-shock batons and cattle prods with shotguns and shells.[9]

Amnesty International and the Federation of American Scientists challenged the US government to reveal which items had been exported to each country. The US Commerce Department refused but, in response to letters from the public, the US Secretary for Commerce stated that his Department had never, nor would it ever, issue export licences for "specially designed implements of torture".[10] It remains unclear exactly which items fall within this definition — at present only one item, "thumbscrews", is listed as indicative.[11]

[9] Federation of American Scientists, *Arms Sales Monitor*, 20 July 1995.

[10] Federation of American Scientists, *Arms Sales Monitor*, 5 March 1996.

UNITED STATES OF AMERICA

Commercial confidentiality continues to be used to justify secrecy in this area. Unpublished data leaked from the US Commerce Department shows that electro-shock weapons were licensed for export to several countries where Amnesty International has documented electro-shock torture, including Argentina, Indonesia, Mexico and Saudi Arabia.

There is no sign that the trade in electro-shock equipment has been curbed. One investigation of US Commerce Department documents in April 1998 found that "a dozen shipments of stun guns and shock batons" had been approved "over the past decade to Saudi Arabia".[12] In 1997 a US-supplied remote control electro-shock belt was being tested in a maximum security prison in South Africa, a country with persistent problems of torture and ill-treatment by members of the security forces.

The USA has also supplied electric shock devices to Mexico despite persistent reports of electro-shock torture. In September 1997 the Mexican "Cobra" security force sprayed water and used electro-shock weapons against peaceful demonstrators protesting against election fraud in Campeche.

Data on export licences issued by the Department of Commerce does not provide a complete picture because many transactions do not require a licence. For example, US exports of law enforcement equipment to Turkey, like all NATO members, are exempt. In addition, despite US law, US companies have arranged supply outlets through third countries. According to police in the United Kingdom (UK), a London trader supplied 200 electro-shock batons from the USA to the Cyprus police, evading a UK ban. Other US companies have supplied electro-shock weapons to Saudi Arabia legally through the UK, and to Romania using illegal routes through Paris, France, London, UK, and Luxembourg.

The USA has exported small arms and riot control equipment, such as tear-gas, to Bolivia, although reports of serious human rights violations have persisted. During April 1998, members of the Bolivian police, army and Mobile Patrol Unit (UMOPAR) fired on demonstrators supporting a general strike. At least 10 people were killed and dozens injured, including women and children, and tear gas canisters were thrown into a school, affecting several children.

---

[11] Export category OA 983, Federal Regulations, 25 March 1996.

[12] Douglas Waller, "Weapons of Torture", *Time Magazine*, 6 April 1998.

Giving away US arms

Military aid by the USA takes many forms, and in some countries gifts from the US government of military and security equipment contribute to ongoing human rights abuses.

Covert supply operations

Successive US governments have conducted covert arms supply operations, despite the human costs. Past US covert operations, such as those in support of armed opposition groups in Afghanistan during the Soviet invasion of the country (via Pakistan), Angola (via former Zaire), and Nicaragua (via Honduras and El Salvador), have provided weapons and training to forces responsible for large scale human rights abuses.[13] Small arms have spread to surrounding countries many years after they were originally delivered, fuelling continuing violence.[14]

Often these operations are only gradually revealed through the work of investigative journalists and human rights defenders. In 1997, the US government released documents relating to the Central Intelligence Agency's role in training the Honduran security force responsible for acts of torture, including rape, and the "disappearances" of over 100 suspected opponents of the government. A senior Honduran training officer claimed in 1995: "The Americans brought the equipment. They gave the training." The US government also acknowledged paying informants known to be responsible for human rights violations in Guatemala.

Surplus weapons

Since 1990 the US government has given away more than $8 billion worth of "surplus" equipment from US military stocks, including 4,000 heavy tanks, 500 bombers and 200,000 light arms. Recipients in 1996 included Bahrain, Colombia, Egypt, Israel, Jordan, Mexico, Peru, and Turkey.

The US President also has "emergency drawdown" authority to hand over US weapons. This authority has been used to provide substantial military aid to Bosnia-Herzegovina and Jordan, as well as helicopters to Colombia, Israel and Mexico.

---

[13] See for example Michael McClintock, *Instruments of Statecraft: US guerilla warfare, counter-insurgency and counter-terrorism, 1940-1990*, Pantheon Books, 1992.

[14] For example, see *Report of the Panel of Governmental Experts on Small Arms* in "General and Complete Disarmament: Small Arms — Note by the Secretary General of the United Nations", 27 August 1997, A/52/298.

The Israeli Defense Force used US-supplied helicopters to carry out unlawful and indiscriminate killings of civilians in Lebanon during its 1996 operation "Grapes of Wrath".[15] The Colombian and Mexican armed forces have reportedly used helicopters in support of counter-insurgency operations. Serious human rights violations have been committed against civilians during such operations.

Counter-narcotics programs

Counter-narcotics programs have emerged as a major and growing area of US military assistance. The US Congress approved $230 million of counter-narcotics aid for 1998, mainly for South American countries. Much of this aid is in the form of a wide range of lethal weaponry. Some has been given to governments whose armed forces have been responsible for gross human rights violations.

What type of training?

Thousands of foreign military officers are trained in the USA every year and US armed forces conduct training programs and joint exercises around the globe.

The School of the Americas (SOA), located in Fort Benning, Georgia, is the best known US training facility, but it is only one of more than 150 centres in the USA and abroad where foreign officers are trained. A number of SOA "alumni" have been implicated in gross human rights violations. US officials maintain that current trainees are vetted to exclude human rights violators and that courses now include human rights training.

Mexican military officers recently trained by the USA have been accused of gross human rights violations. For example, members of a counter-insurgency force set up in 1994 and known as GAFE (Air-Mobile Special Forces Group) were in military custody at the time of writing, accused of killing one man and torturing several others in San Juan de Ocotán, Jalisco state, in December 1997. GAFE officers have been trained by the US 7th Special Forces group in Fort Bragg, North Carolina; their training reportedly included helicopter assault tactics, explosives, rural and urban warfare. During 1997, 328 Mexican army officers were trained there and subsequently assigned to GAFE units.

The US government has acknowledged that parts of seven Spanish-language training manuals prepared and used by US officials as

---

[15] Amnesty International, *Israel-Lebanon: Unlawful killings during operation Grapes of Wrath*, July 1996 (AI Index: MDE 15/42/96).

recently as 1991 encouraged the use of murder, coercion and ill-treatment. Other similarly disturbing manuals have also come to light. US officials refused to discipline those responsible for producing these manuals on the grounds that there was no "deliberate attempt to violate" US policy.

More than 100,000 foreign military personnel from over 100 countries have received training under the International Military and Education Training (IMET) program since it was established in 1976. Even more are trained under the Foreign Military Sales program. IMET for Indonesia was cut after the 1991 Indonesian army massacre in East Timor. In 1995, Congress agreed an IMET program for Indonesia limited to training in human rights and civilian control. However, in March 1998 leaked official documents revealed that the US government had secretly used another little-known program — Joint Combined Exchange and Training — to train the Indonesian army, including its notorious special forces command (*Kopassus*). Training included close quarters combat, sniper techniques, demolitions, psychological operations and urban operations. US combat troops were involved in at least

© Tami Chappell/Reuters

The School of the Americas, one of more than 150 centres in the USA and abroad where foreign military and police officers are trained. A number of officers trained at the School of the Americas have been implicated in gross human rights violations.

41 such exercises between 1992 and 1997, and 20 more were scheduled for 1998, despite continued reports of human rights abuses by the Indonesian security forces.[16]

Several US companies with close links to the US Department of Defense are now offering military training and other services that used to be provided only by governments. For instance, a US company has received a substantial contract to help train and organize the armed forces of Bosnia-Herzegovina. In Saudi Arabia numerous US companies are training every branch of the armed forces. In 1998, one US company had over 1,000 employees in Saudi Arabia, mostly former US army and special forces personnel, to "modernize" the National Guard, a force responsible for internal security.[17] In October 1997 another US company describing itself as a "defense contractor" sent about 500 retired US special force personnel to the Cabinda enclave of Angola, where civilians are engulfed in a prolonged armed conflict and serious human rights abuses. Sometimes, both US government and private military contractors have provided training and other support for foreign armed forces whose members are committing human rights abuses. This was the case for example in Rwanda from 1996 to 1998; Amnesty International has sought clarification of the US role there.[18]

Accountability

Several US laws regulate the international transfer of military and security equipment and expertise. Under the Arms Export Control Act, the State Department (Bureau of Political and Military Affairs) must approve all foreign weapons sales. Under the Export Administration Act, all exports of dual (civil-military) use equipment and technologies, and law enforcement equipment, are controlled by the Commerce Department. Human rights concerns, regional stability, non-proliferation and other issues are considered, along with the potential impact on the US arms industry. Decisions are generally made on a case-by-case basis, and in mid-1998, 24 countries were under some form of US arms embargo including Afghanistan, Myanmar (Burma) and Indonesia (light arms prohibited).

---

[16] Alan Nairn, "Indonesian Killers", *The Nation*, 30 March 1998.

[17] David Shearer, *Private Armies and Military Intervention*, International Institute for Strategic Studies, Adelphi Paper 316, 1998.

[18] Amnesty International, *Rwanda: Ending the Silence*, 25 September 1997, (AI Index: AFR 47/32/97).

Under Section 502B of the Foreign Assistance Act, the US is required to cut off all security assistance to any government which "engages in a consistent pattern of gross violations of internationally recognized human rights" unless the US President deems that there are "extraordinary circumstances". However, Section 502B has never been used to cut off such aid. Likewise, the US Congress has never formally blocked a sale proposed by the US executive branch, although a few sales have been delayed, modified or withdrawn.

Both the US Commerce and State Departments are meant to run programs to verify that sales are going to declared buyers and are being used for legitimate purposes. According to the State Department, foreign governments receiving arms and security equipment from the USA commit themselves to use it "solely for internal security, for legitimate defence, for participation in regional or collective (defense) arrangements or for measures consistent with the Charter of the United Nations". However, information is rarely made public on end-uses which violate international human rights standards and international humanitarian law. Even less is revealed about the activities of private US arms brokers and private military training firms even though they are required under US law to register with the US State Department.

All arms brokers and private military training firms are required under US law to register with the US State Department and both the US Commerce and State Departments run programs to verify that sales are going to declared buyers and are being used for legitimate purposes. However, insufficient information is publicized to allow full scrutiny by Congress or the public.

Recently, the US Congress adopted a new provision known as the Leahy Amendment.[19] This prohibits the USA from providing most forms of security assistance to any military or police unit when there is "credible evidence" that members of the unit are committing gross human rights violations. Assistance can resume if the government in question takes "effective measures" to bring the responsible individuals to justice. How effective this new provision will prove remains to be seen, but it is currently undermined by inadequate end-use monitoring.

---

[19] Senator Patrick Leahy amended the Foreign Operations Appropriations Act (FY 1997) in September 1996 to prohibit US counter-narcotics funding to units of foreign security forces implicated in gross human rights violations. The second "Leahy Amendment", passed in November 1997, enabled all aid covered by the Act to be prohibited to units of foreign security forces implicated in gross human rights violations.

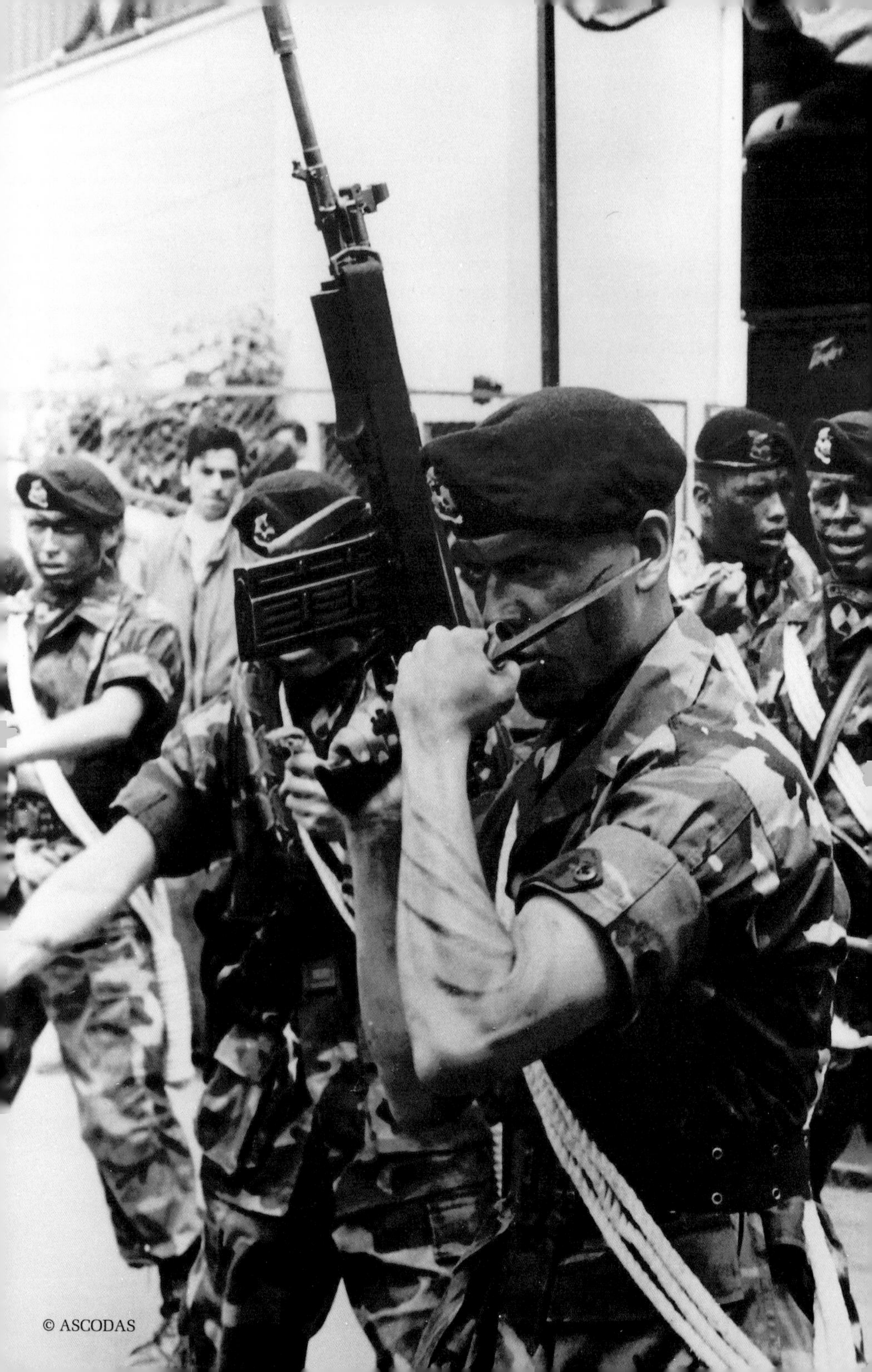

International controls

In today's global markets the most effective way to ensure that international arms transfers do not contribute to human rights violations is by international agreement. Since the USA is by far the largest supplier, it has a duty to provide a lead.

On 30 May 1997, Amnesty International joined 14 other Nobel Peace Prize Laureates in proposing an International Code of Conduct on Arms Transfers, and the European Union adopted a code of conduct on arms exports in June 1998.

The US House of Representatives passed a proposed national Code of Conduct to regulate conventional arms transfers in 1997, but it has not yet been adopted by the full Congress and has faced opposition from the US arms industry. Under the proposed US Code, weapons can be transferred only to states which meet criteria in four areas: human rights conduct; non-aggression; democratic government; and full participation in the UN Register of Conventional Arms. The proposed Code gives the US President responsibility to seek international agreements to secure arms control using the same criteria. A weakness of the proposed Code was that it allowed the President to waive its provisions if required by national security or emergency, even though Congress may overrule the President. Another weakness was that it covered conventional arms and international military training, but not law enforcement equipment or training.

Recommendations

In order to reinforce the USA's stated commitment not to contribute to human rights abuses in other countries through the supply of military, security and police equipment or expertise, certain immediate changes are necessary in US law and its implementation. Particularly in light of its prominent role in the global arms market, the US government should:

1. Provide clear, detailed, regular and comprehensive information about all prospective and completed transfers of arms and security equipment, technology, expertise, training and services by both private companies and government agencies. All companies involved in such transfers to foreign customers using third countries should be

Left: *Members of a Colombian army counter-insurgency unit. Amnesty International members in the USA have campaigned to prevent military aid being supplied to the Colombian armed forces without adequate controls.*

publicly registered with a US agency and subject to the same rules as those that govern all transfers from the USA.

2. Adopt a binding Code of Conduct, based on international humanitarian law and international human rights standards, to monitor and control all US transfers of military, security and police equipment, services and expertise. All proposed transfers, including those brokered through third countries and those involving licensed production arrangements in other countries, should require prior public scrutiny and approval. If there is good reason to assume that a transfer will contribute to human rights abuses or breaches of international humanitarian law, it should not be approved.

3. Strengthen the capacity to monitor the end uses of US transfers of military, security and police equipment, services and expertise in order to ensure that if such transfers are subsequently used to facilitate human rights abuses or breaches of humanitarian law, further supplies of such transfers can be stopped. All end-use certificates should require recipients to undertake in advance not to use the transfers for human rights abuses or breaches of international humanitarian law; failing this the contracts for the supply of those types of transfers can be rendered null and void and further equipment, spare parts, training and repair services halted.

4. Prohibit the manufacture and export of equipment solely used for executions or for torture or cruel, inhuman or degrading treatment (including remote control electro-shock stun belts). Suspend the manufacture, use and export of any type of equipment where credible evidence has shown that it may inherently lend itself to human rights abuse, pending the outcome of a rigorous, independent and impartial inquiry into the use and effects of that type of equipment.

5. Promote the inclusion of the above provisions in international binding agreements. Sign and encourage ratification of the Convention on the Prohibition of the Use, Stockpiling, Production and Transfer of Anti-Personnel Mines and on Their Destruction (the Ottawa Convention).

9

RIGHTS FOR ALL:
Time to deliver

There is a persistent and widespread pattern of human rights violations in the USA. Across the country thousands of people are subjected to sustained and deliberate brutality at the hands of police officers. Cruel, degrading and sometimes life-threatening methods of restraint continue to be a feature of the US criminal justice system. In US prisons and jails inmates are physically and sexually abused by other inmates and by guards in overcrowded and under-staffed prisons, many of them privatized. Sanctions against those responsible for these abuses are rare.

Many people who have been forced by persecution to leave their countries and seek asylum are held behind bars, for indefinite periods, in conditions that are sometimes inhuman and degrading.

More than 350 prisoners have been executed since 1990. Some were children when the crimes were committed; some were severely mentally impaired. Another 3,300 people are on death row, put there by a system whose application of the death penalty is arbitrary and subject to racial and class bias.

Amnesty International is calling on the USA to end these violations of the right to freedom from torture and cruel, inhuman or degrading treatment, the right to freedom from arbitrary detention and the right to life. The US government has so far been reluctant to ratify international human rights standards which guarantee such basic rights, and to bring US law and practice into line with these standards. Taking such steps would be a clear signal of its intent to ensure human rights for all its people.

As a leading supplier of arms, security equipment and military training, the US government has an obligation to ensure that there are systems in place to prevent the export of this equipment and expertise to governments or armed groups which will use them to carry out human rights abuses. In the absence of such controls, the US government and US companies continue to supply human rights abusers with the means to continue violating fundamental human rights.

UNITED STATES OF AMERICA

Amnesty International's campaign on the USA aims to increase public awareness, both within the country and internationally, about the denial of certain fundamental human rights to many in US society. In this it seeks to complement and support the work of the thousands of human rights activists and defenders in the USA and to increase and strengthen cooperation with the human rights community.

Amnesty International is making a number of recommendations[1] to federal, state and local governments to increase accountability on human rights issues and achieve some concrete reforms which will help bring an end to these abuses. These recommendations include: increasing the accountability of the police by setting up effective oversight and monitoring mechanisms; establishing enforceable standards for the treatment of prisoners, including steps to prevent sexual abuse of women and a ban on the use of remote control electro-shock stun belts; an immediate end to the execution of juvenile offenders and the mentally impaired, and a moratorium on executions, as steps towards abolition of the death penalty; an end to the detention of asylum-seekers in jails; ratifying international human rights treaties in full; and adopting a code of conduct to prevent US arms and equipment being used to commit abuses elsewhere in the world.

The USA has been quick to voice its condemnation of human rights violations in some other countries and to stress, by contrast, the wealth, of civil and political rights which it guarantees within its borders. As this report shows, however, it has failed to deliver these rights to many of its people and there are signs that, unless urgent steps are taken, these rights will be further eroded.

It is with a sense of urgency, therefore, that Amnesty International is launching a major campaign on human rights violations in the USA. The organization's members around the world will be working to promote international human rights standards, to stimulate debate about human rights in the USA, and to publicize the organization's concerns as widely as possible. They will also be urging US federal and state authorities to implement Amnesty International's recommendations as a clear and public affirmation of a renewed commitment to placing human rights protection at the heart of US domestic and foreign policy.

The USA's contribution to the evolution of our understanding of basic human rights is a remarkable part of its national inheritance. Yet

---

[1] For detailed recommendations on each issue, please refer to the final section of the relevant chapter in this report.

the promise of human rights for all people, spelled out 50 years ago in the Universal Declaration of Human Rights, remains unrealized for sections of US society. Central to the concept of human rights embodied in the Universal Declaration is that human rights cannot be guaranteed selectively. If one right can be violated with impunity, then so can another, and perhaps with even greater ease. If one person can be denied their basic human rights, for whatever reason, then it is that much easier to deny those rights to someone else.

The call for greater respect for human rights in the USA is part of a campaign to promote those rights for all people in all countries.

If you wish to add your voice to the call for rights for all, join us in our campaign.

APPENDIX:
Selected Amnesty International reports on the USA

Forthcoming reports

Amnesty International plans to issue reports on the following issues during the course of its campaign for Rights for All in the USA:

The death penalty and innocence

Juvenile justice — human rights violations and children

Death penalty and the mentally ill

Death penalty and race

Detention of asylum-seekers

Women

Selected Amnesty International reports

Police

AMR 51/36/96, *USA: Police brutality and excessive force in the New York City Police Department*

AMR 51/76/92, *USA: Torture, ill-treatment and excessive force by police in Los Angeles, California*

AMR 51/26/87, *USA: Allegations of ill-treatment in Marion Prison, Illinois*

Prisons

AMR 51/51/97, *USA: Ill-treatment of inmates in Maricopa County jails — Arizona*

AMR 51/02/96, *USA: Florida reintroduces chain gangs*

AMR 51/135/95, *USA: Reintroduction of chain gangs — cruel and degrading*

AMR 51/35/94, *USA: Conditions for death row prisoners in H-Unit, Oklahoma State Penitentiary*

AMR 51/34/88, *USA: The High Security Unit (HSU), Lexington Federal Prison, Kentucky*

Refugees/asylum-seekers

ACT 34/03/98, *Refugees: Human rights have no borders*

AMR 51/86/94, *USA/Cuba: Cuban "rafters" — pawns of two governments*

AMR 51/31/94, *USA/Haiti: The price of rejection: human rights consequences for rejected Haitian asylum-seekers*

AMR 51/07/94, *USA: Forcible return of Haitian asylum-seekers by the United States*

AMR 51/31/93, *USA: Failure to protect Haitian refugees*

POL 33/06/93, *Refugee protection at risk*

Death Penalty

Amnesty International produces annual reports on "death penalty developments" in the USA.

AMR 51/27/98, *USA: The execution of Ángel Breard: apologies are not enough*

AMR 51/20/98, *USA: "A macabre assembly line of death"*

AMR 51/14/98, *USA: Ángel Francisco Breard: facing death in a foreign land*

AMR 51/10/98, *USA: The death penalty in Texas: lethal injustice*

AMR 51/01/98, *USA: Violation of the rights of foreign nationals under sentence of death*

ACT 50/02/98, *Juveniles and the death penalty — executions worldwide since 1985*

ACT 50/01/98, *Lethal Injection: The medical technology of execution*

AMR 51/25/96, *USA: The death penalty in Georgia: racist, arbitrary and unfair*

CHAPTER 2

ACT 51/2/95, *The death penalty: No solution to illicit drugs*

AMR 51/146/95, *USA: Guinevere García: a case of state assisted suicide*

AMR 51/07/95, *USA: Follow-up to Amnesty International's open letter to the President on the death penalty*

AMR 51/89/94, *USA: The case of Gary Tyler, Louisiana*

AMR 51/01/94, *USA: Open letter to the President on the death penalty*

AMR 51/74/93, *USA: Texas: Executing juvenile offenders*

AMR 51/46/93, *USA: Imminent execution of juvenile offenders*

AMR 51/26/91, *USA: Federal death penalty — 1991 crime bill*

AMR 51/23/91, *USA: The death penalty and juvenile offenders*

AMR 51/19/89, *USA: The death penalty — The risk of executing the innocent*

AMR 51/01/87, *USA: The death penalty*

Other US reports

AMR 51/03/98, *USA: Human rights concerns in border region with Mexico*

AMR 51/25/95, *USA: Human rights violations: a summary of Amnesty International's concerns*

AMR 51/31/92, *USA: Human rights and American Indians*

AMR 51/27/88, *USA: The case of Elmer "Geronimo" Pratt*

The annual *Amnesty International Report* summarizes human rights developments in the USA during the preceding year.

Other relevant reports

IOR 51/01/98,*"Old enough to kill but too young to vote": Draft optional protocol to the Convention on the Rights of the Child on the involvement of children in armed conflicts*

ACT 40/01/97, *Arming the Torturers: Electro-shock Torture and the Spread of Stun Technology*

AFR 47/32/97, *Rwanda: Ending the Silence*

AMR 34/02/97, *Guatemala: State of impunity*

EUR 45/06/97, *UK Special Security Units — Cruel, Inhuman and Degrading Treatment*

EUR 44/84/96, *Turkey: No security without human rights*

IOR 30/06/96, *APEC: Human rights and development*

MDE 15/42/96, *Israel-Lebanon: Unlawful killing during operation Grapes of Wrath*

ACT 75/03/95, *Psychiatry: A human rights perspective*

AFR 20/03/95, *Chad: Empty promises: human rights violations continue with impunity*

ASA 11/09/95, *Afghanistan: International responsibility for human rights disaster*

EUR 44/01/95, *Turkey: A Policy of Denial*

MDE 15/15/95, *Israel and the Occupied Territories including the areas under jurisdiction of the Palestinian Authority: Trial at midnight: secret, summary, unfair trials in Gaza*

AMR 36/33/94, *Haiti: On the horns of a dilemma: military repression or foreign invasion?*

AMR 29/12/93, *El Salvador: Peace without justice*

IOR 41/33/93, *Statements to the 45th session of the UN Sub-Commission on Prevention of Discrimination and Protection of Minorities*